MASTER OF ONE

A SOUL MAP FOR CONSCIOUS LIVING

MASTER OF ONE

A SOUL MAP FOR CONSCIOUS LIVING

BY
JACQUELINE TEEJ

the kind press

Copyright © 2020 Jacqueline Teej

First published by the kind press, 2020

All rights reserved. No part of this book may be reproduced, stored in a retrieval system or transmitted in any form or by any means, electronic, mechanical photocopying, recording, or otherwise, without written permission from the author and publisher.

The author of this book does not dispense medical advice or prescribe the use of any technique as a form of treatment for physical, emotional, or medical problems without the advice of a physician, either directly or indirectly. The intent of the author is only to offer information of a general nature to help you in your quest for wellbeing. While the publisher and author have used their best efforts in preparing this book, the material in this book is of the nature of general comment only. In the event you use any of the information in this book for yourself, the author and the publisher assume no responsibility for your actions.

Cover and images by Jess Lee Williams
Interior layout by Elle Lynn

Cataloguing-in-Publication entry is available from the National Library Australia.

NATIONAL
LIBRARY
OF AUSTRALIA

ISBN 978-0-6485917-4-0 (Paperback)
ISBN 978-0-6485917-5-7 (Ebook)

Dedication

To the awakened soul
who is ready to light up the path of wherever they walk,
and light up the hearts of others. The world is ready for you.

Never stop believing in the wild possibility that is you.

Live in purpose. On purpose.

Dear readers,

These words are an energetic transmission to lay the foundations for a better understanding of the journey of your soul and the nature of the Universe.

It's the desire of the soul to grow, learn and expand. Your life lessons are filtered through the cycle of your soul which is illuminated throughout the *Master of One*. Each part will help you navigate through life in your truest essence and aligned purpose. This can be depicted through the soul cycle of initiation; our awakening; transition; transcendence and to the blossoming of self-actualisation. It is intended that you see your life unfolding throughout each chapter, to see where you might be on your journey and to assist you in staying true to who you are. This book is about *you*.

No matter whether you're in synchronistical flow or if you're a chaotic mess, you can see how all is perfect for you in this moment. Choose to see this book as a soul map. Here to guide you when you need it. Your map will look completely different to another, but when you're lost, unsure about what's happening or where to go next, see your life reflected through the chapters. With each heartfelt intention to help you align to your highest calling and to anchor you back in your authentic truth. Allow the soul map to merge with you. Assisting you to find love, peace and acceptance within your heart and to help you uncover the life you were meant to live.

After you have finished reading each chapter, you may want to pause and reflect. No one can step into a completely new way of thought, dimension and transcendence and comprehend it all at once.

Always remember that this is new knowledge and therefore has a new language. As you read on, what you will find is profoundly simple and a new way of being. It will become a part of you.

After you read this book, you may wish to go back from time to time until you begin to wonder why you could ever have thought any other way. *Master of One* will lead you to your soul's calling, what you read in words are recorded upon your Spirit from Source and goes beyond your mind and into your consciousness, you will become all that you are—"I AM."

Keep an open mind and heart as you merge with a higher consciousness and connect with the magical unfolding of your unique journey.

CONTENTS

Wisdom of the soul   xv
Introduction   xvii

PART I - INITIATION

Wake Up	4
Your Time is Now	6
Self-Discovery	11
Your Soul Blueprint	16
My Initiation	20
Initiation Summary	24

PART II - AWAKENING

A New Awareness	28
The Sign of Awakening	30
A Shift in Perception	35
Dark Night of The Soul	39
Unconscious to Conscious	42
Identity of The Self	44
Alignment Through All Realms	46
Spirituality	48
Awakening Summary	54

PART III - TRANSITION

Universal Flow	60
You Won't Know Until You Let Go	62
What Do I Need to Shift?	65
Accessing Higher Guidance	77
Healing	79

A Sacred Practice	84
The Void	88
The Missing Years	90
The Universe is Working for You	97
Transition Summary	99

PART IV - CHANGE AND INTEGRATION

Soul Alignment	106
Getting in Sync	108
Breaking Co-dependency	113
The Spiritual Ego	115
It's Not Your Job	120
Get Grounded	122
Authentic Living	125
Honour Yourself	128
Growing Through Challenges	132
It's Okay Not to Be Okay	136
Coping with Drastic Changes	138
The Drama Storm	142
The Divine Presence	144
Increase in Sensitivity	149
Energetic Boundaries	152
Energetic Self-Care	159
Energetic Detox	163
Forgiveness	166
Change and Integration Summary	172

PART V - TRANSCENDENCE

Simplicity	176
Spirited Life	179

Your Sacred Gifts	182
Integrity	189
Honour Your Journey	191
Your Physical Body	193
Expanded Consciousness	197
Spiritual Influencer	199
Life Purpose	201
Balancing Energies	204
Who Am I?	206
Universal Spirit	211
High-Vibe Commitments	213
How May I Serve Today?	215
Unleash Your Destiny	217
Your Soul Call	219
The World Needs You	222
Match Your Intention	224
You Shall Receive	226
The Power of the Heart	229
The Zero Point	232
The Next Step	234
Transcendence Summary	236

PART VI - SELF-ACTUALISATION

Lessons for Your Soul	242
Master Thyself	244
Light Way	249
Divine Aspects	251
Divine Connection	253
Divine Mind	256
Divine Heart	260

Divine Creator	265
Divine Purpose	271
Divine Presence	280
Self-Actualisation Summary	283
A Blessing	*287*
Soul Mastery	*289*
Soul Map	*298*
Acknowledgements	*306*
About The Author	*309*

"Lord, make me an instrument of your peace.
Where there is hatred, let me sow love;
Where there is injury, pardon;
Where there is discord, union;
Where there is doubt, faith;
Where there is despair, hope;
Where there is darkness, light;
Where there is sadness, joy.

O divine Master, grant that I may not so much seek
to be consoled as to console,
to be understood as to understand,
to be loved as to love.
For it is in giving that we receive,
it is in pardoning that we are pardoned,
and it is in dying that we are born to eternal life.
                                                   Amen."

WISDOM OF THE SOUL

Trust the process.
Live authentically.
Laugh a lot.
Believe in the power of your dreams.

Your talents and interests will give you guidance towards what your life calling is. Navigate through life as your best Self. The past has served its purpose, allow it to be a lesson. Love. Take the risk of love. Love every part of yourself. Be fearless in what you believe in. Take moments to pause and be still. Start and end your day with gratitude. Listen to wise words. Experience helps. Spend less time *selfying* and create more moments to capture in your heart. Travel. Find yourself, who you truly are. Speak and spread kindness. It always has a ripple effect and will come back to you in greater magnitude. Leave nothing left unsaid or undone. Forgiveness is the strongest action we can show. Love, even if it's not always reciprocated back. To know you've loved is what matters most. Spend your energy to those whom are worth your focus and time. Time is a currency we don't get back. Make your life profitable by making high-vibe commitments. Don't settle for anything less than what you deserve. You are worthy of all good things to come your way, even if your ego makes you think otherwise. Be committed in the process of transforming your mindset. Be humble. Be *in* integrity. Stay aligned to your authentic Self. Support others. Create financial abundance by choosing to save and spend on quality things that make your heart open. We come into this world with nothing and it's what we leave this world with, nothing. Material possessions aren't what gives us fulfillment, it's the quality of life that we live. Keep your imagination and childlike heart open. Every fingerprint is unique just as you are. You are the change the world needs. Try your best to master your mind, emotions and body. This is the only element of real control you have in your life. Be of true service to yourself and to others. Have the courage to pursue the desires of your soul. Be you, after all, your true nature is an expression of the Divine.

Be the Light. You are the Light.
Know thyself. This is your soul journey.
You are already home.

Welcome.

INTRODUCTION

I wish someone gave me a manual on how to navigate through life with this new expanded awareness that came through my first spiritual awakening. During phases in my life, I felt alone. I didn't know what to do or who to turn to. I turned inward, even though I was never shown how. I couldn't just open up a book to get the guidance I needed to fulfil my life's calling or how to deal with adversity. I would get on my knees, begging the Universe to show me signs and answer my questions, 'Who am I?' 'What am I meant to do?' 'Why is this happening to me?' I often felt as if the Universe wasn't listening. As I continued along my spiritual journey, I found more and more people awakening, going through the same experiences, deep processes and feelings. I noticed that people would enter into my life at critical moments in *their* life where they needed to move forward on their soul journey.

That is how this book *Master of One* came about. I would write about what I was experiencing at the time and it naturally unfolded into the blossoming cycle of the soul's evolutionary process and how to activate your true soul's presence each day. I didn't know how this book was going to turn out. As a teacher, I would always encourage my students to write using a process, this is not how the book came about, actually it was the complete opposite. Teacher's love that sense of control and when you live by spirit, well, it's completely out of your control. When you think about it, the path of the soul is illogical. We can only do our best in each moment to be ready and willing to act out our soul's impulses. I knew in my heart that there was an urgency to write. It wasn't until almost completing the book that I saw how everything just made sense. I trusted in a higher power to flow through me and I had to ensure that I created this in the right energy. The words in this book are an energy. An energy for alignment, healing and peace for your mind, body and soul. We might not end our journey being fully self-actualised, we are part human after all, but this is about how we can call in our presence in each and every moment when we might be going through chaos or even success. How can we stay more in the presence of our heart and soul? How do we fully step into the power of Light? And when we feel off, how can we come back to our centre?

Every human, whether perceived 'awake' or not, will experience in their life some form of awakening to align them to their highest calling. Some of us have more of a heightened sense of awareness than others. When we experience traumatic events, challenges or difficulties, we are being pulled more to our true Self, our divine Self. These circumstances don't arise to push us away from the Divine, but rather to find the avenues to bring us closer to Source. Who am I if I'm not the person I thought I once was? When your perceptions become shattered, it can cause turbulence to our ego and our sense of identity. Our life can feel like it's in crisis.

How can you stay aligned when you might be going through a deep emotional time or you're going through some crazy circumstances? What are you meant to do when your life has completely turned upside down? If the Universe is loving and all providing, why would we have to experience any sort of pain? Until I learnt what was going on and how to trust, I would find that I would experience extreme emotional and circumstantial polarities.

We are learning how to bridge between heaven and earth. Balancing extreme polarities. We are learning how to integrate both our physical and divine aspects, our soul. It's imperative for both of these aspects to be balanced. Being more of one world, constricts the ability for magic and miracles to work in your life. Without our human nature, we can't connect with others and ground our magical flow. Without our spiritual essence, we miss the beauty that the Universe is always providing us. We are all an expression of the Divine, living our unique life purpose. We are all doing the best that we can in each and every moment. Every moment is an alignment to your calling.

Throughout the book, I use the words the Divine, Source and the Universe as the ultimate presence that created every particle, every atom and every *thing* that ever existed. It's an infinite and abundant energy of unconditional love and peace that is all around us. I can't describe what the Divine is for you and you can't name that which is mystical—you can substitute *it* for what feels right for you whether it's God, Goddess, Deva, there is no right or wrong—substitute it for the word that makes your heart expand.

Being guided by a higher power, to follow the light, is the new way. With each conscious action that we all decide to take, we lift the vibration of humanity. This is the time of the rise of the Lightworker. We are no longer hiding in the shadows but facing the world without fear. If there is even an ounce of fear, we are learning to move forward with courage and conviction. We are co-creating a space where only love exists because the actions of heaven are one of love and support.

We are all being called to be more of our *true* Self. Each part of our journey is leading us closer to our true nature, to our home. When we show up as our true Self we inspire others to show up as their authentic Self. This ignites a light in their heart to spread onto others. This is why your work is so important. Your presence is needed. Each inspired action you take in the presence of your soul is creating the greatest shift in the collective consciousness. We are the shift in humanity. We are shifting lifetimes of ancestral habits, thoughts and actions that are not aligned with our divine nature. There's no coincidence why so many people are awakening at this potent point in time where we are undoing all actions which are not part of the Earth's true blueprint. Our inner and outer worlds will become a reflection of what our true state is. We have a long way to go until this could become possible, but it's only through being courageous to follow the impulses of our soul that we can make the impossible, possible.

My intention for you throughout this book is to discover ways in which you can stay in flow. The flow of your soul to live out your highest calling. To assist you through your deepest and darkest times and to live in hope knowing that you are fully loved and supported by something greater than you could ever imagine. You can enter a chapter which you feel you're experiencing at this time in your life or you can enjoy the journey from start to finish. You could even use this as an Oracle and open up the book to a page you need to receive a message on. There's no right or wrong. Follow whatever your heart desires. I know that as I write this book, this book becomes a constant evolution like a reflection of the journey of the soul.

**We are healing together, collectively.
We are coming back to our true birthright on
reclaiming our divine humanness.**

You are a beautiful soul living a human experience, entrusted with a divine assignment only you can fulfil. This is your calling. Let's heal and shine together. Welcome back home.

On behalf of all of the Universe and your Guides, thank you for being you and all that you do. You are so loved and supported unconditionally with whatever actions you choose to make.

**With love, light,
peace, gratitude.**

PART I
INITIATION

Welcome Initiate

Initiations are the gateway to the Divine.

WAKE UP

Welcome to a different world you never thought possible.

A new way of being.
Every initiation comes with a deep purpose.

Initiations are erratic. Like childbirth, we are unaware when the exact moment is going to happen, but the soul knows. Your guides know and are prepared to support you on your journey. You can't predict the exact time, but that seed has been planted since before your birth. Every new upcoming phase in our life comes with an initiation. It can come in many forms. Like the birth of anything, it can be painful, but the blessings are there if you keep persisting.

We can't see it, but there's an invisible force slowly stirring in us ready to be expressed. Our initiation is this invisible force piercing through. The Universe is shaking you up and your perceptions to welcome you into a new way of thinking and being. Your shake-up and wake up, is providing the path for *you* to lead *you* to your destiny. The Divine has been calling you and now is your time to listen and answer.

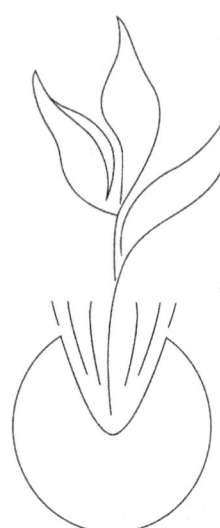

THE DIVINE CALL IS UNPLUGGING YOU FROM THE ILLUSIONS OF LIFE.

YOUR TIME IS NOW

Can you recall a moment in your life when it truly changed the whole course of your life? You may have experienced something deeply traumatic, or an erratic shift in perceptions or interests that set you on a completely different path that you never thought was possible. When was that moment for you? Maybe it was losing a loved one, being in a toxic relationship or experiencing a debilitating circumstance. Did it shatter you so much that you had no choice but to surrender to a higher power? Initiations provide the gateway for the presence of your soul to shine through more into your life. It is a Divine destined moment which was meant to occur.

New initiations in life come about like an earthquake—shattering what you thought life was about—and opening you up to explore a new realm of possibilities. They have to come through this way. You can navigate through life with uncertainty and ambiguity, without a GPS or a manual on how-to-get-through-this-life. When the world you once knew has been broken down of all its illusions, all you have with you is faith. Faith that you will be led to where you need to be in all the uncertainty. The Lightworker is birthed. It's been within you all this time. How you shine your light differs to another. The actions you decide to make after your initiation matters.

The *now* is the only time to create a better future and that better future exists now because of every single conscious choice we, the collective, make. Never underestimate every good deed you do and how that impacts humanity. When you choose to act from the space of love and peace, you are passing on the light for others to follow. That's why we are being initiated, expanding our awareness, so that we, as a collective, light other hearts to act in the same way. My dad always said, 'Be kind to everyone you meet, because you never know when you might need them.' Even though it's not always reciprocated, I always found that having a good heart, allowed others to act from their heart too. People don't forget how you treat them.

I was in a leadership position at a school and it was time to reapply for it. There was no other person suited for the role. I loved my work and was passionate about it. I remember going into the office and meeting my boss. He told me I didn't get the position because someone with more experience was coming back to the organisation from maternity leave and they needed to offer her the leadership position back. I was devastated because I knew the person taking it wasn't going to do the role justice. She wasn't passionate about wellbeing like I was. Usually when I'm met with disappointment I cry or dwell on it for at least a week, but something was different this time. I could've just lost it, all that hard work I knew was going to be undone, but I chose to come from a different perspective. One of peace, acceptance, gratitude and love. There was some niggling feeling and peace in my heart that this needed to happen. I had worked on my processes so much after being constantly met with challenges and this time I didn't want to come from a place where my ego was dented. I chose to come from the space of the heart, and I know that my reaction made an impact on my boss at the time because he said to his assistant later on that you can tell the type of person I am by the way that I handled myself. There was a shift in our relationship after that experience and he became one of my biggest supporters, especially when I moved on from that workplace. He was like my big dad in the working field. I thanked him for the opportunity and experience that it had provided for me. He was worried that I would've been upset or angry. I didn't have any of those feelings. I know that every door that closes becomes a chapter in your life that's complete and when this happens, the Universe is asking you to flow somewhere else and this is *okay*. My time there was done. It was time to move on. My time to shine my light somewhere else was a new beginning and that was exciting. It gave me permission to move on and that's the closure that I needed. Initiations are the clue that a new beginning is about to happen, and we are about to embark on an important lesson in our journey for our soul's evolution.

Although, you will hear about my initiation soon, I want to point out the importance even the smallest actions can make. It's the micro moments that matter. It was my initiation into something new and I had the full support of my boss which was imperative for me in moving forward. My positive conscious reaction, came from working through my 'stuff' for many years and I know that when you come from the heart space, it provides the greatest shift for others to shine. No matter how insignificant you think it might be. I didn't realise at the time, but the Universe was pointing me in a different direction because I had some inner work to do. Now, was the time for me to move because I had a soul mission to complete and it was no longer at that workplace. I had broken through resisting change to embracing it. That chapter was now done. It was my time to act and right now in this moment, you too might be going through the same. Maybe your chapter is done and now a completely new book of your life is awaiting to be written.

There has never been such a greater point in humanity to make the shift other than now. I wish I could tell you that there might be just one shocking initiation that might occur but many of us are constantly being initiated into higher states of awareness. When we are ready to transcend our consciousness, we become initiated again to bring into our awareness anything that's either not from a higher perspective or to shift our focus on a completely different aligned path. As one door closes, another door opens. The more we open up to a higher power, the more light and heart expanding experiences we are being asked to uphold.

Do you think your initiation was by mistake? No way!

SOUL MASTERY LESSON

* Your initiation is perfectly orchestrated for you to change your life.
* What was your great initiation that set you on a new path you never thought possible?
* Be as open as you can when you're being initiated into a new journey to allow the Universe to flow through you.
* You are being asked to move forward in a new direction.
* Thank yourself for all that you've done for yourself and others.
* You are beginning a new cycle in your life.

YOU TRULY ARE AMAZING!

SELF-DISCOVERY

What brings you into feeling whole and complete? I know that every time my life has gone to shambles, I have to detach, pick myself up and drag myself to become functional again. I travel, get creative, treat myself and get back to what I know brings me joy. Every initiation shakes the core of your being so that you become clear about what it is that your soul truly strives for. Whatever we do in life is a result of what we believe we are.

We can continue to walk our path to seek a deeper meaning to life and to feel a sense of divine purpose. We want to matter in this world, we all matter regardless of what we have or haven't done. Some of us can feel in our hearts that we are here to create a legacy and make an enormous shift in the collective consciousness. We can spend our lifetime discovering who we are and trying to decipher what this world is about. We can spend our lifetime with regret on things we choose to do or not do. We can wonder what our life would be like if we chose certain actions or didn't let fear get in the way. Each action we take is determined by what we know about ourselves. Our identity is the key to what actions we take in our life.

Who am I?
What am I meant to do?
How do I fit in?

It's a never-ending quest to find that missing puzzle piece that makes our life feel complete. Yet, there is a yearning deep within our heart and soul for us to feel whole and complete. Do we feel complete and whole in a lover's love? Alone? With our children? Working in a job? What is it for you that makes you feel whole? What gives you a sense of complete oneness? There are more unanswered questions than solutions to this life we know of. You can find that people who have all the money in the world, still suffer, yet those with very little are satisfied. You can get married and have kids because you've been told that this is true fulfillment. There are many people who might've acted in this way before they were ready because they were told that this was the way to be and find that they're unhappy. The ideal dream didn't turn out the way it was expected. For some, this is what happens perfectly, and it brings so much joy, happiness and fulfillment.

Our initiation is asking us to illuminate our lives in truth. How can we get the desired answers we are after if it's not through becoming *enlightened* in some shape or form?

> *En:* to cause or be in
> *Lighten:* illuminate, radiant energy, unveiling the Light

Through this, we can see that we unveil the Light within all situations. You can't be in this present moment right now without an experience of some spiritual awareness that's been bestowed upon you. Enlightenment is an initiation into the Divine. The Divine chooses your time. It has nothing to do with your doing. Everything has been perfectly orchestrated before you entered this earth plane.

I think we get a clue about enlightenment through ancient stories that have been passed down from many generations and by many religions. Each place in the world has important concepts of what makes up the Divine, yet the Divine is not a construct of the mind. The Divine is what it is. It can't be named. It's as if little droplets of the Divine are present in every ancient story, sacred place and tradition whispering to us, saying, "This is how you can live in a self-actualised state in this world." If we choose to pick up the essence of what each story brings, we can begin to unfold a greater sense of life, direction and purpose. Our ancient ancestors gave us the greatest cues to live the best life possible.

If you have been awakened, you cannot go back to the way things were. No matter how hard you try. What do you do? How do you make sense of all the chaos? How will you lead this world with this new perspective? You could hide. However, destiny will not allow you to shrink away. What good is an awakened awareness without being able to work with it? It came for a reason, in that moment, for a reason. If you feel it hasn't happened for you, the fact that you're attracted to this book is that it's happening to you right now or it is coming.

Our enlightening process, if birthed too quickly brings a big shock to the system. That sort of awareness can be hard to take all at once. Immense suffering can influence your ability to feel connected and have faith in the Divine. Your true nature of joy and pure bliss could be awakened to a world that feels completely different to the flow of the Divine. Our physiology and brain wouldn't be able to handle all of this new information and awareness. Life feels that it is not the same, nor ever will be. It's not meant to be. It can't be. You become unplugged from the matrix of life. Your friends, family or interests may leave you and a complete change of career may come up for you. You've started a new genesis chapter in your life. That pivotal moment means that it was the right time for your soul to awaken so that it can give you the greatest influence on your life path. So, what do you do with this new sort of knowledge? You can never go back to your naïve state. You feel again like that baby learning how to walk, learning how to work through the polarities through transcending a new level of awareness. With great power and knowledge comes great responsibility.

The greatest shake-up we receive are our perceptions—that have been blinded by illusions—awakened to Spiritual Truth. Our level of Spiritual Truth is at the level of how much our soul's growth has occurred throughout our lifetimes. We take this with us in each reincarnation. Our perspective on life must change if we are to change the world. What is good or bad is only the meaning we place on it. A 'bad' experience can open us up to what we deserve, the good in life. Being in a bad relationship can show us what we want in a partnership next time. There is a greater divine plan beyond our comprehension, we just have to show up in each moment to flow with it.

In each struggle there is a blessing waiting to unfold. As challenges present, my friend Nicole would always end with, '. . . this too shall pass.' Temporary pain has the potential to unlock a lifetime of bliss if you're willing to follow the path of your heart, even when it makes no sense at all to do so. Follow the flow of your heart and it will lead you to unlimited blessings. Sometimes, challenges will come your way to unlock you to more flow and allow more of you to shine. However, everything that we experience in life is predetermined before we even came through to this Earth place.

. . . THIS TOO SHALL PASS.

YOUR SOUL BLUEPRINT

Each and every one of you has a special and unique purpose in this lifetime. We have all been allocated divine assignments to work through and lessons to learn. Before coming into this lifetime, you orchestrated everything you'd like to experience with your Master Guide: this is a divine being who oversees your soul's growth and what you need to experience.

Do you think that everything that has happened to you was by chance or a mistake? Every person and every experience were made for you. Those who challenge you, love you so much on a soul level that they wanted to help you evolve a karmic lesson that you may have struggled with or want to master in this lifetime. If we only could see the perspective of our soul and get a glimpse of our Soul Blueprint, we could see how everything makes sense. Our Soul Blueprint contains every single detail of what we are going to experience in this lifetime. It includes our gifts, lessons and any contracts we have with others that we need to make amends with. If we knew every single detail about what was going to happen during our existence, life would be boring.

However, most people are not privy to this insight into their Soul Blueprint, it unfolds during their journey. We can get little snippets of it. If we could understand what we signed up for, everything would make sense. We would never question any experience. We would know that this is what our soul wants to experience, and everything will actually be okay. As hard as it is, pain is where our soul is given an opportunity to expand, that's if we are willing to do the work to transcend the pain. Sometimes, we are the catalyst for someone else's experience because on a soul level we love them so much that we knew we were strong enough to help their growth.

Before we enter this physical realm, we check in with the souls' that we are choosing to incarnate with in this lifetime. We become equipped with all the knowledge, skills and talents that we have used in many multiverses and lifetimes that are beneficial to use in this reincarnation, or there are some new souls being birthed that have never incarnated before on Earth and they have gifts that can be utilised for humanity as well. Like a seed planted, everything you need sits inside of *you*—you may not be able to see it, but it's there beneath the surface—it's a part of you. It becomes a part of your physical DNA. You can call upon these gifts at any time. As you begin to live an embodiment of your soul essence into human existence, you will begin to awaken your divine potential and unlock more of the true you that lives out your highest potentiality. These gifts become even more apparent once you've been awakened to a deeper sense of awareness because they are your interests or skills that come naturally to you or evolve over time.

When we are born into this world, we forget everything and our sacred mission. If you don't know what your life purpose is, that's okay. If you're unclear about what you're meant to be doing in this life, life will unfold for you. I know that it can feel frustrating. I know I've had many times where the call feels like loud screams coming from within but when you reflect on the now, where you want to be and where you are don't appear to be congruent. However, to live out your life purpose, the key is to go where you feel your heart expands. You already have everything you need inside. We might not understand why we might feel compelled to be somewhere, see someone or do something, but trust that with each heart expansion, flow will begin to enter your life. These important lessons through all these interactions gives us clues to what we are meant to be doing in this lifetime. With every action step we begin to light up our Soul Blueprint which contains all the information that we need to know in this lifetime about what our life purpose is. Only when you're ready, the right lesson and experience will appear.

If you're experiencing the same toxic cycle or attracting the same people or experiences, then this gives you an insight into what lessons you're learning to master in this lifetime. There is a particular theme which might keep reappearing in your life. Be mindful of this. Your awareness of your thoughts, patterns, actions and reactions will help you to change the influence that this lesson might be having in your life. I know that there have been many occasions where I've personally thought I've transcended a lesson, and boom, there it shows up again. Your mastery is determined on how you choose to act with this same lesson. Our reaction to whatever lesson unfolds for us is an indicator on whether or not you have transcended your thoughts, perceptions and processes to a higher state of consciousness. The more we learn to master our lessons, the less detached and emotionally charged we feel towards them. They're meant to trigger a part of you to grow. If it challenges you, you are evolving, and your soul is striving to constantly evolve. That's what is contained in your Soul Blueprint after all.

SOUL MASTERY INQUIRY

* If fear wasn't an option, what would you do in your life?
* What comes naturally to you?
* What are your gifts and talents?
* What do you enjoy doing in your spare time?
* What would your ideal life look like, where are you, who surrounds you?
* What opens your heart?
* What is a main theme in your life that you feel has been a big lesson for you?
* What has challenged you?
* Right now, what do you feel you need to let go of?
* What do you feel is the next step for you?
* What do you feel you're meant to do?

MY INITIATION

Your initiation might come differently to mine and that's how it's meant to be. When I tell people about that exact moment in time that my initiation occurred it can sound unthinkable. If I told the story of what happened to me to myself ten years ago, I wouldn't have believed it either. I guess the Universe wanted to make an unbeliever, a believer. Everyone will experience their own sense of initiation perfectly for their soul's evolution. I ask you to come with an open mind towards my initiation which undoubtedly made me step into a faith of something greater than what I can see. After my initiation, I couldn't go back to the life I lived and that started me on my spiritual journey.

It was a Tuesday night.
I had gone to receive my second Reiki session. Home, feeling quite relaxed, I went to bed early. Before I continue, please, don't think that if you're going to go to a Reiki session that this is what will happen to you. This was orchestrated in my Soul Blueprint to happen this way. Yours can happen differently and perfectly. I don't want any of you who have never had a Reiki before to think that this is the norm that occurs.
I woke up in the middle of the night and my whole body was paralysed. Yet every cell in my body was vibrating, surging with energy.

I heard an incredible deafening whooshing sound as if I was outside on the runway at an airport. I could see different images like I was travelling through other dimensions. I was jumping through rainbow portals through the stars, going from a dream into a dream. I know, I sound crazy right now. I prayed. I prayed to all the angels I knew. I had no idea what was going on. I was so fearful but curious. It all ended with a silver-like angel flying through my room. Google couldn't give me the answers. Some would say this is astral travelling. My mind was blown. From that moment on I knew that my life would never be the same again.

In the morning when I woke, I could still feel the energy and electricity surge throughout my whole body. I had no idea what had happened. I had never felt anything like it before. I messaged my friend that day to ask her what had happened to me. She was the only one I knew on the spiritual path I could talk to. No-one else in my life had gone to have Reiki before. *Was this the norm?* I felt like I had been reborn. I was experiencing new senses for the first time. But instead of this being like a baby with no awareness of the world I was an adult with a mind that loves to overthink! I had no idea how to control the energy that was buzzing through me. I kept zapping people and the things I touched would become zapped too. I felt like the superhero, Shazam.

I ended up getting in contact with the therapist to ask her what had happened to me. She had mentioned something about it being a part of my ascension process and back then I had no idea what that even meant. *What does ascension even mean?* I Googled that too. I just wanted a clear-cut answer about what was going on. Why was I feeling electricity all around me and feeling energy surges through my hands? Why was I paralysed in bed jumping through portals? Why did I wake up and feel so light as if I was walking through the air? *Have I reached a moment of insanity? Did I die? Is this heaven?* I write all of this now and I might sound crazy, but I know some of you will be able to relate. And even if you don't relate that's okay, trust me, anyone who has had an initiation knows that it can feel quite bizarre and out of the blue. It's meant to shock you. It has to startle you in some form. How else can you receive an expanded awareness unless you've been able to see things differently?

I find that the 'Initiation Stage' gives you a sense that the Divine is at play. You'll receive what you need to help solidify something that is tangible but can't be recreated by you. It might be feeling heat, tingling, a synchronicity, or an overwhelming feeling of change. My initiation woke me. It helped me to bring an awareness of what was not in alignment to the surface and changed what I valued in life. I know that after my initiation my life was never the same again. I couldn't go back to my old life. My friends who I had a superficial relationship with left. My relationships with others and my thoughts about my career had completely changed. I was no longer that person living in the illusion that wasn't congruent with my soul essence. As hard as it was this is what needed to happen. When you've completed a cycle in your life, get ready for your next initiation.

INITIATION SUMMARY

Your initiation was orchestrated before you incarnated onto this Earth. This is in your Soul Blueprint. Everything you need to navigate every situation in this life is in your DNA. Like a seed the clues you are after are already within you. Each time you unlock an important aspect of your life it unlocks within you the awareness for what you need next, slowly drip feeding into your consciousness. If you were born with the awareness of everything you needed to experience, life would be boring. What would be the point? Your life is literally a choose-your-own-adventure with unlimited possible outcomes.

Your uniquely tailored blueprint is carried within you, in your consciousness, to be accessed at the right moment in time to give you exactly what you need. The lessons you need to experience in this lifetime are necessary. Learn how to master your lessons by becoming less reactionary. Your initiation was needed to unveil an awareness that something is needing your immediate attention. A soul integration needing to be made and a change that is congruent with your life purpose. An initiation is the Divine made present. Be aware that something greater is assisting you to shift into your divine presence. Your initiation is an acknowledgement of a new phase in your life.

PART II
AWAKENING

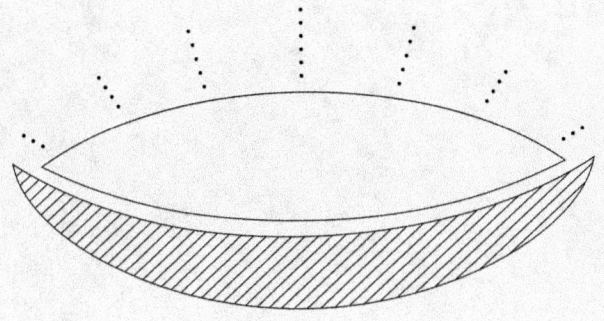

Become Awake

We are here to awaken from our illusion of separateness.

—THICH NHAT HANH

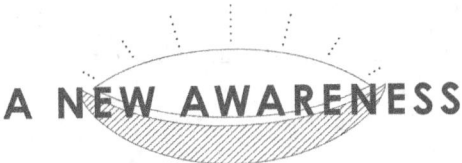

A NEW AWARENESS

Do you know who you are and where your life is meant to go? Without conscious awareness of who we are, what our soul desires are and where we are heading, we can become lost in a sea of expectations of where society wants our life to flow. However, your awakening becomes the discovery of who you truly are and what you truly want to manifest within your heart. It is illuminating for you all that is in the way of you seeing the truth.

Awakening to a new awareness gives you clarity of what is *not* aligned with your spirit. It begins the process of allowing you to consciously move towards what is congruent with your soul and what you need to do to live out your destiny. But where do you start?

It becomes the undeniable process of understanding what might be some of your attachments, illusions and all that which is not allowing you to flourish and shine in this moment. Maybe you have a feeling in your heart that something is going on, but you might not be sure what it is just yet—this is where your synchronistical signs amp up—or the insights may come to you instantly. Our shifts in awareness become a shift in perception as well because they need to. If our perceptions shape our thoughts, behaviour and reality, then awareness becomes the light that pierces through your consciousness for greater change. It becomes pivotal for your soul journey. Your soul no longer wants to stay dormant, it's awakening, and it is time to stop hitting the snooze alarm and allow it to rise within you, starting with your awareness.

> ### SOUL MASTERY INQUIRY
> * What new awareness is rising within you now?
> * List all the times in your life where you have had something major happen to you. Write them down and think about what change they brought about for you. This can be good or something you found extremely challenging. Do you notice any themes? What new awareness did it awaken within you?

THE SIGN OF AWAKENING

Know that when you're initiated, your awareness expands. When your awareness expands, this becomes an awakening to something even greater. This is the signal of your awakening. Whether you're in the initial stages of your journey or a well-established traveller, the signs will continue to flow to let you know that something beyond your control is about to happen. To happen for your highest good, even when it's the opposite to what you're truly feeling. This could include feeling like there are coincidences; like thinking of someone and they call, seeing repetitive numbers, finding quotes on social media that are exactly what you need to read, finding coins or seeing butterflies, the signs are endless. It can feel strange. You can't deny that something bigger is at play! Your rational mind would think that it is really just a spooky coincidence, but you know that you can't deny that there is something grander happening in the bigger picture. This part of your journey is truly when you don't know where you're headed or what to experience, but you know deep down that something is happening. Don't think that you're in this all alone. Let me tell you, Spirit is always checking in on you and helping to orchestrate the signs to come your way.

As you look down at the clock or at the environment around you, do you notice any repetitive numbers like 11:11, 111, 222, 333 and so on? Is it just a coincidence or is there another reason that each day you could see the same repetitive number without even knowing the actual time? The Universe is trying to grab our attention for something greater. It is bringing our awareness that what we desire is coming our way or what we need to pay attention to. Numbers are an easy way for the Universe to communicate with you.

THE SPIRITUAL MEANING OF NUMBERS

1

Stay positive. Positive abundance energy.
Creation.

2

Stay alert. Keep your thoughts in check,
stay focused on what you want.
Duality. Balance.

3

You're fully supported.
Creativity. Outcomes.

4

Angels surround you.
Foundations.

5

Change. Challenge. Freedom.

> **6**
>
> Grounding. Magical. Practical.
> Relationships. Love.
>
> **7**
>
> Divine. Metaphysical.
> Meditation. Self-reflection.
>
> **8**
>
> True abundance. Finances and experiences.
> Great creative energy. Infinite. Manifestation.
>
> **9**
>
> Endings. End of a cycle.
> Completion.
>
> **0**
>
> Reset. Infinity. Cycle.

If you keep seeing a particular sequence of numbers, combine the numbers to see what message you may receive. They may be a message for Spirit to get your attention. Numbers might mean something different to you. You decipher what it means for you. This is just a general guide.

And what is so special about 11:11? Some believe that this is a special moment of a gateway to healing and positive energy. I always take a moment to close my eyes, breathe, thank Spirit for guiding me along my journey and make a wish for all the things I desire in my life from aligned intentions. The signs that are sent to us no matter how they appear mean that we are on another phase of our journey that requires us to be alert and even though we might not know where it's flowing, we are already sailing in the boat of our life path, being guided and directed and the Universe is saying, "We are here for you!"

SOUL MASTERY INQUIRY

* What signs are you seeing in your awakening phase?
* What numbers are you constantly seeing?
* What do they mean for you?
* Are you ready to embark on a new adventure?
* Can you sense something is happening but you're not sure what?
* What do you feel is a coincidence, spooky or keeps happening?
* What signs do you think the Universe is sending you?

TAKE TIME TO NOTICE THE SIGNS.

A SHIFT IN PERCEPTION

If you're reading this book, you would be able to pinpoint a time which turned your life around and sent you on a quest you never thought would've even entered your consciousness. This moment in time shattered an aspect of your perception on the world, it opened your awareness to something greater, so that you could create purposeful action in the world. If a part of your lifetime lesson is to gain enlightenment, it means that there's a point in your life that will send you over the edge, it may even happen a few times. I can't tell you how many *Dark Nights of the Soul* times I've had!

Your awakening can come in many different ways and it differs for everyone. You may even experience somewhat that it can only be described as miraculous or feel like an out of body experience. Even if you feel as though you haven't had the feelings of 'an awakening', the fact that you're drawn to this book is a gateway to your own unique awakening. You don't choose when you'll be awakened, it's already destined for you. The universal life force that flows through you, chooses for you.

For me, my awakening came in a ripple effect. It started for me when

I decided to go for a Reiki session. I had heard that there was this amazing holistic practitioner who was psychic and would give a reading during her sessions and a lot of people who went to her found that whatever she said had come true. Before entering this space, I was not awakened at all. Still stuck in what society wanted me to be, I was disempowered, unaware and passionless. I was stuck in a relationship I felt trapped in. I wasn't enjoying work at all but knew that I needed to work to pay the bills. What was I meant to do? I was brought up that you go to school, university, get a job that will be your career for your *whole* life, marry, have kids and then life would be fulfilled. I thought I had it all figured out. It was what was told to me by my external world. Maybe I had chosen wrong and I was stuck in this prison life.

When I walked in, the first words she said to me were, 'You're such a beautiful soul, but is your work really making you happy?' Work was on my mind. It wasn't making me happy. That was the first time I had actually stopped to reflect and talked to someone that it wasn't fulfilling me, so I was intrigued to hear every word that she said. During the session, she picked up on things that I hadn't told another soul. I'd never been so open and vulnerable before, but it was also a relief in a way to have someone understand every part of me without having to say a word. As I was quite a secretive, private person with trust issues, this really blew my mind. For me, this was the turning point in my life. I was unconsciously walking in pain and all of a sudden it was if a new perception had filtered in which allowed me to see the power that I had in my life. I began to call my power back. From that moment on, was when I began to unravel what I could only describe as crazy, beautiful, challenging and divine.

There's always caution, of course. Once you're awakened, you can never go back. This is the challenge. How can you bring your awakened Self to show up each day? Some days are harder than others. Some days I feel like I come from another planet. I know many of you can relate. Where you can feel that this level of awareness can be more of a burden than a blessing? Then there are times when you might feel that no-one can relate or get it. This is when we need to start calling in and meeting people who are like-minded so that we don't need to do the journey alone anymore.

It can feel easy to navigate through life by just going through the motions—to do your mundane job, live out the perfect life—but when the calling in your heart gets loud, move. But we shouldn't wait until the pain in our hearts become unbearable. You do have the power to create any change in your life and it might just start with shifting your perceptions. Your initiation into a greater awareness on life is to show you the endless possibilities that is presented in front of you. Once, just strolling through life can now feel like what you see isn't exactly what it's meant to be. The issue is the questions that arise. *Who am I? What am I meant to do?* When we live by the conditions of what society has wanted us to be, we can feel that life becomes meaningless. This is because meaning has been constructed from a cerebral level, not on a soul level. This is a time when we are truly beginning to tap into Spirit fulfillment. Know that when you show up in the world as your authentic Self, this is already doing wonders for the world. That's purpose in action.

SOUL MASTERY INQUIRY

* Have you experienced some form of deep pain or trauma that made you go on a quest of self-discovery?
* Do you feel different from others, sometimes feeling alone and

that no-one understands you?
* Are you drawn to a particular spiritual practice or something completely out of the blue that you've never experienced before?
* How has your thoughts and perceptions changed on things since your awakening?
* What idea, thought or perception do you feel needs to be changed in order to follow your soul?

DARK NIGHT OF THE SOUL

The wound is the place where the Light enters you.
– RUMI

Our first dark night of the soul is one of the hardest experiences we ever have. The intensity of the emotions can feel unbearable. Our emotions can override our feeling of connection. A transition occurs as the death of the ego leads to the awakening of the heart. We may feel arise uncontrollable emotions and body shaking. A sense that life is out of control—deep trauma—as the removal of the illusion we live is revealed. This aspect of our life isn't to be feared. It's through the darkness that we move closer to the light than we think. A Divine intervention has been placed in order for you to awaken to your divine potential and bring sacred union to your soul. That particular moment has been orchestrated from your Soul Blueprint for your awakening to occur.

When I reflect back on my dark night of the soul experience, it was when I had given my power away to another and placed my focus on something that was toxic for my being. It shadowed my ability to do what I needed to do. I needed this shake-up. Without it, I'd still be stuck. I couldn't stop crying. It consumed my thoughts. I had felt that someone was literally ripping up my soul. I know this sounds a bit dramatic, but I was being asked to let go of someone that was extremely toxic for me. I had to let them go, but I didn't want to. I was holding on to the addiction of them. My mind was consumed with what I was letting go of instead of focusing on what was coming in.

If we are really invested in anything that isn't soulful, the Universe will come with its big scissors and say, 'Now is the time to cut this out of your life.' Like a loving parent, Spirit always has our back. If you can't see the patterns, habits or experiences that are holding you back, they will intervene. You can see that your divine assignment is too important to be wasting it on nothingness. Your soul may have requested it. The first time can always feel the hardest because it is our first experience with this immense deep pain. Don't lose hope if you're going through this right now. You *will* lose your sense of Self—you're meant to—you're meant to lose the identity of what the world taught you to be. You are shaken up because the person and the world you thought that was true, is no longer the illusion you perceive it to be. What will you do, or can you do? Trust yourself. Gather the strength to keep going. It is such a dark period in your life but it's the unveiling of your diamond within.

As you continue on the journey, you might find you have multiple experiences of this deep transformational period. Even though it can be quite traumatic going through this period multiple times, stay with a hopeful heart as it means that another aspect of your life that is no longer serving you is you leaving and it finally has the shake-up it needs to exit your life. It is the cord that is holding you back that needs to be released. You are allowing more space for the Light to enter. The dark night of the soul is bringing to light what is rising in you—the unconscious—to your consciousness. It is all for a divine purpose. It can last a few days, weeks to even a few months. You have enough strength and courage to get through this. If you're going through this right now, then you are detaching from anything that doesn't bring the unity of your true spirit and it's making way for this union to occur. You've got this.

> ### SOUL MASTERY LESSON
> As you experience a dark night of the soul remember to stay centred knowing that this is for a divine reason. Be willing to release this deep pain or trauma from your being. It might be hard to see it now but find the treasure from this experience. This comes through time. Whatever is happening to you, ask, is it helping you to move forward in your life? Give yourself time to heal.

UNCONSCIOUS TO CONSCIOUS

Everything that is hidden will become revealed. Our awakening process unlocks the process of the unconscious to conscious. It's like waking up from a dream where you lived in oblivion. Every moment moving forward seeks to make each present moment amplified with focused conscious awareness. This consciousness will eventually lead you to the true essence of who you are, the I AM consciousness. The more you begin to strip away the aspects of your ego that presented itself as your unconscious Self, the deeper and higher you go into your expanded awareness. We *break* into our soul consciousness. This is a higher state of awareness. The blocks to flow are lifted and provide shock to our being to a fully awakened conscious being.

Who are you if you're not attached to your story? These attachments to your past—the story that you believe makes up your identity—is what can stop you from experiencing your true essence, your divine presence. Breaking into conscious awareness means that you're becoming more conscious of your divine Self and the mission of what you're truly here to do. Tap into that flow. That stream which flows throughout the Universe. The unconscious operates from a mental and emotional layer. The conscious operate from Spirit. They embody the Spirit element. Your suffering offers the opportunity for transcendence. This is a shift of consciousness. Transcendence offers the opportunity for more light to come in. So, we tap more into the universal presence that surrounds us always.

Your *I Am Presence* is formless.

As your unconscious slowly becomes undone, your eyes and physical being are brought into a deeper awareness of the true Self, the I AM presence. Your formless presence. Not the presence you conceptualise with your mind. Formless, effortless flow. It is only through asking yourself, 'Who Am I?' are we able to tap into a deeper sense of higher consciousness. Your essence identity.

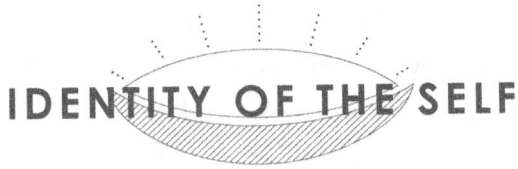

IDENTITY OF THE SELF

Who Am I?
Why am I here?
What am I meant to do with my life?

These are the most common questions that people will ask themselves. You may be asking this about yourself. We all are driven by a sense of purpose and our human conditioning is that we need to feel like we belong.

Your awakening is the slow release of your Ego Self, towards your divine Self, your best Self. When we are born, we are told who to be. We understand our world through how we have been brought up—from our family, environment, schooling, community and circumstances—all influencing how you perceive to operate in the world. We are governed by rules and we understand what is *good* or *bad*. Think about your parents for a moment. Have you adopted any qualities from them? Have you ever heard you're more like your father or mother? Who are you if you weren't the person you were told to be? What would you be doing? What would your life be like? Maybe you had such a bad experience growing up that you decided to be the complete opposite to what they were.

When we are awakened, we are unplugged from our programs and it is as if we are navigating our life like in the movie, *The Matrix*. Your awareness on all that is happening around you seems to be on slow-mo. These programs can be inhibiting you from living your best life as your best Self. It's the program that keeps you attached to things that are toxic for your being. When we ask ourselves *Who am I?* We're asking on a deeper level *What is my true identity? What is my true Self?* This Self exists not from our stories we have accumulated over the years or your experiences or what others or even you think about yourself—that is a limited perception of the Self—the true Self exists in the paradigm of an unlimited stream of consciousness, an expanded sense of awareness. This limitless being where anything is possible.

Stripping your entire ego in an instance would cause a healing crisis within your being. It's why the journey expands over your lifetime, not just in a single moment. If we were purely of Spirit, we wouldn't be able to understand the world entirely. A balanced mind is one which can translate, think and act in accordance with Spirit. We are updating our mind to think more from our Highest Self, than lower thought forms.

Your Highest Self is the absence of judgement and the presence of love. It is an extension of Source. We are all an extension of Source. We become lighter as our conditioning and attachments fade away. Our perception begins to change, from a limited perspective, to a wise one. We understand and embody more of who we truly are, rather than just merely, our humanly identity.

ALIGNMENT THROUGH ALL REALMS

The whole world is going through a major shake-up, an identity crisis. We have seen the rise of humanity coming either as one or against one another. There are two polarities existing. Those who seek peace, love and equality. The other power and control. We are rising as one to be the change. A rise where we have begun to develop a conscious awareness of the true blueprint of the planet. Within each individual—unconsciously—they contain this seed. Awake or asleep, every single person has the power to change. The chaos reflects where the change is needed. It shakes up our values. Who you were five years ago or who you identified with would be totally different to today?

When we have our awakening, our earthly identity will constantly keep evolving. We get closer to our Higher Self, the best possible evolution for this reincarnation in this lifetime. As triggers occur that rock our foundations, we get clues about what our Spirit stands for. This is a powerful understanding. This transformative period becomes so powerful that you can no longer live out of integrity or feel like you can connect with others who are *out* of theirs. This is okay. Your interests, commitments, experiences will only reflect more of what is of value to you. Follow it. You are a divine being who has experienced many lifetimes of developing gifts and talents and your accessing that unlimited capacity of your being now.

> **Check-in: are you in alignment of Self in all aspects of your life, or do you hide away in certain areas?**

Just take a moment to look at social media and you can take a glimpse into someone's world or perceived persona. With the rise of the digital age, we have a crisis of:
Who am I in a spiritual sense, my true nature?
Who am I in this physical reality?
Who am I in this virtual reality?

Are you in alignment in all realms of life or do you portray to the world one aspect of yourself, when you're really another? Live a life that's congruent with your soul and your values. Perhaps there are aspects in your life you feel like you want to hide? They could be because of work purposes or you're not entirely out of the spiritual closet yet. There are some circumstances where you may feel you need to protect your identify, this is okay as long as you're not sacrificing your essence for the approval of others. Who you are is good enough.

SOUL MASTERY INQUIRY

* What do you value in life?
* What and who do you feel makes you compromise who you are?
* Are you able to be authentically you in all areas of your life?
* What actions do you need to take to come into full alignment?

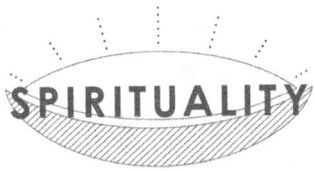

SPIRITUALITY

Writing this part is important and I'm sure many of you can relate to what I'm going to write next. Before reading on it's imperative to do what feels right for you. To believe in what's right for you on your journey. Spirituality may be viewed as a chapter that challenge's the ego—know that each and every word is coming from the heart—I'm asking you to come with an open mind to a topic that has become clouded and ambiguous. I want to bring more light, appreciation and acceptance to the sacred aspect that connects us to a greater presence. We have to navigate through illusions to see what may be perceived as being separated from the Divine. You can stay stuck in the cycle of co-dependency or learn to connect to a higher power in your own way.

Our sacred journey is a spiritual experience—we are *all* spiritual beings—you are a spiritual being having a human experience right now. As you walk the path, you empower your divine Self in this present moment more and more. That's why, I think it's really important to talk about spirituality. What does spirituality or being spiritual mean to you? Over the past decade, the spiritual industry has boomed. Meditation which was once thought of as something that only monks do is now accepted as the norm. Even top professional sporting organisations are embracing the power of meditation and yoga. There is power in the sacred practice of ancient traditions.

The rise in the spirituality industry has meant that there have been many seeking a spiritual knowledge and truth. It has also meant the filtration throughout the years has gained a mentality of *us* versus *them* which is a form of separation. At the emerging stages of this spiritual movement, freedom and wholeness were encouraged. However, instead of the expansion feeling of love and flow, some seekers have felt that they have received judgement on Self and others from those who are an expert in the field.

The biggest part of going to church or a religious organisation is to build a community, because you need to have some form of support when you have a faith in something greater. That's why the spiritual journey can feel lonely. Often, a journey for the seeker is akin to living like a hermit trying to access that inner guide. Each and every person's awakening is different to another. Every person who walks their path will experience something completely unique to them. That's why to truly define what a spiritual person is differs from person to person. To have a truly spiritual experience is to feel the divine presence in your life. This can be experienced whether you are a part of a religious or spiritual association or not. Religious organisations have allowed us to live up to certain values or morals that shape how society acts and behaves. One key theme that is expressed through all religions is that it always comes back to love. Love is always the answer and the answer of the Divine for humanity to live in harmony.

Being spiritual encourages you to find a deeper sense of presence within yourself. To experience the divine, rather than listen to the stories that influence your understanding of it. Stories that are in religious organisations have strong moral messages, but over time some strong influencers changed the interpretation of the stories to reflect what that society was going through in that particular time. You can experience the Divine without having to be in a certain physical structure or initiated in a certain space through ceremony. Your initiation comes through being of the world. There's no discrimination. We learn from those stories that Source is experienced through life. If we left sacred texts unfiltered through interpretation, we could see the diamonds that exist within each sacred word and the true messages to remind us how we are truly meant to live each day.

Through choosing to live a spiritual life, you develop your inner GPS for guidance by discovering for yourself how this extraordinary divine presence shows up for you each day. By using all your senses, you will understand and feel how the Divine speaks to you in each moment. Acting in a way that might seem unnatural to others, yet it all makes sense to your mind and Spirit. How simple it actually can be, yet paradoxically difficult as you try to understand the ultimate question of existence that we all ask ourselves: Who am I? The deeper you dig, the knowledge you receive can be beyond your comprehension. As it may serve a purpose, not all things should be taken as direct facts. As it appears, parts of the spiritual industry have lost integrity and authenticity. People are coming in with great egos, preaching love, yet are driven by power and greed. Again, no different from a cult, driving forms of unconscious manipulation to force people to follow, rather than to trust their own sense of inner knowing and self-worth. The benefits of religious organisations are that there are clear guidelines on how to be a part of a religion. However, in the spiritual industry there aren't any set of rules to abide by which creates ambiguity and grey areas.

Live by kindness. I want to say love, but love can mean something different in all cultures. Unless you understand in your heart unconditional love and the real meaning which is treating others with kindness and accepting them for who they are, whatever actions they choose to make. You have to know clearly what is true to your heart and true spirit. We are talking about a unified Universal Law.

Find what feels true to your being in this moment. If anything is less than simple, then that truth can be misguided. We can feel a sense of something greater in our lives. Whether it is we believe that we are Pleiadean, Starseeds, Atlantean, an Angel or have multi-dimensional aspects, this can be great knowledge and you could have some past-life flashbacks from certain aspects of your being. But how can this truth help you to connect with humanity when you truly want to be of service? How can someone connect with you if you ostracize yourself as a certain aspect? It can sometimes make you feel lonely and alienated. It could also bring in for you your tribe. However, if we can accept these aspects of ourselves, they may bring us gifts and lessons we can spread upon this earth which is exciting. I'm not asking that you disregard these parts of yourself if this is in your belief system. It's learning how to integrate this part of yourself in the moment. As this moment is all that counts. Purposeful intentions of the present moment act as the most powerful catalyst for change.

Furthermore, I truly believe there is a need for a code of ethics within the spiritual industry to maintain its integrity. Within all industries there can be manipulation and when we are walking the spiritual path and acting as a guide to many, it's important to come from the heart, not the ego. In divine truth there's no place for using people for financial gain, for receiving financial gain from any form of unethical measures is not honourable in any sense. The moment we become co-dependent on a spiritual leader; we disempower our being. For we are all made up of the same matter and we all matter. Anyone stating that they are the only way, are certainly not The Way. People can only act as guides to assist us when we need them most and show us the way to receive the Divine in many shapes and forms. It's all in your divine blueprint. My intention and hope are that you find the way, strengthen your own trust in your intuition and find the connection of the Universe that flows through you in every moment. The most spiritual person can be the one you perceive as the most ordinary person who is doing an ordinary job. This person comes from the heart and acts with good intentions, integrity and authenticity. This is spiritual.

It can appear that the more ungrounded you are, the more spiritual you are, which is far from the truth. I remember rocking up with jeans and a top to a conscious dance party and I was judged by a self-proclaimed hippy, she was sage smudging the crap out of me as if I was just a muggle. I felt major judgement. She didn't know that I worked hard to clear my energy each day. She judged me for what I was wearing, and I felt ostracized in that moment. Being a spiritual being is not what you wear or have. It's who you are.

The truth is, we have to learn to be the bridge between both worlds. The journey of understanding how to navigate through both worlds brings you closer towards enlightenment and self-mastery. Like walking on a tight rope, we are learning how to balance both worlds. We need to upkeep our spiritual practice to stay connected and we still need to be in the world connecting with people, places and experiences. We need to connect with people at their level of understanding of the world. Ascension is about bringing heaven on earth which is a process of descension. Grounding as much as what you are experiencing along the way as we are the messengers of a higher calling. We are all acting out for a divine purpose and we live out the calling of the Divine through our guided actions. What you experience is for a purpose. If you are truly aligned to the Light, the experiences that you receive is because you become the best at communicating in a way that can help others to find that infinite intelligence that surrounds all of us.

You are the messenger. It's up to you how you decide to interpret and share your insights on what is presented to you. Your ability to share your insights, aligned to the Divine, can help shift the consciousness of humanity which has been entrusted to you. Whether you're writing a post on social media, helping out a friend, or writing a blog, you are consciously choosing the energy you'd like others to receive. Every choice you make is made up of conscious intentions. How will you choose to act as a representative of the Divine?

> Don't be spiritual,
> the act of knowledge.
>
> Be spirited,
> the act of understanding and living in that essence.
>
> **Be led by Spirit in every moment.**
> **You will then know that you are truly divinely guided.**

Your path is unique. Spirituality is an experience that can only be felt, not understood. If you 'understand' spirituality, you misunderstand the experience. This is your awakening. A yearning to reconnect with a deeper presence.

AWAKENING SUMMARY

Awakening can shake and rock you to the core. There might have been no other way for you to see that something needed to change without it happening this way. The truth is breaking free and bringing about a much-needed self-awareness. An awareness of your soul and all that *it* is. Evolution can only happen when we are awakened to what it is that is bringing about conscious or unconscious suffering. The pain can push you out of an illusion that has not been serving you for so long. It can push you out from being stuck in conditional patterning that is not serving your soul.

All that comes to your awareness is bringing you into union with your soul. What's not in union becomes a feedback mechanism through deep emotions and negative thoughts. These are signs that there is something that needs to change, and you might be unaware of what that is now, but that's why it is leading you up to a transitional phase of your life. There's an undeniable force working through your life, piercing through the cracks, aligning you to where you need to go and if you allow the universe to just flow, you'll flow with it too.

The universe will continue to send you signs, little nudges that you're on the right track with encouragement. We have to understand what our unique signs might be. Our awakening is shifting our being to higher thought forms and consciousness. Transitional periods become needed in order to give time for an unyielding conscious awareness to form and to solidify this into your energetic and physical field.

PART III
TRANSITION

Moving from your order to divine order

Be realistic: Plan for a miracle.

—OSHO

UNIVERSAL FLOW

You may need to revisit this part of the book a few times, as there are moments in your life where you may feel that you're in a stagnant phase and not in flow. If you're going through this then it's time to take some time out with your soul and reflect. Contemplate what and where is it that your soul is guiding you to next. Your awareness will awaken you to where you need to be next and what you need to do to become congruent with your soul and your purpose. This becomes a transitional period for you, and it can be quite painful if you're unsure how to navigate through it. It's important to be clear and real with yourself. If you are unable to make time for yourself to reflect where you're going, you may feel stuck. No-one likes that feeling, unless you love the chaos!

Firstly, I want to tell you that you can never be out of flow with the Universe. You can only walk each step with flow; nevertheless, you can feel an extreme resistance to the path you need to travel on. The resistance is pulling you to where you need to be. When you learn to stop resisting, you're able to accept and ride with the current that will ultimately lead you to where you need to be. There are also times where you may feel that you are stuck in a void, neither here nor there going nowhere. It's as if you've lost the Wi-Fi signal even when you know that the router is on. You await to grab onto anything that will show you what direction you need to be at. It is through the void period which your test of faith and ability to surrender becomes prevalent. It's a blessing to solidify your new awakened consciousness within your being.

The Universe is infinite and abundant with endless possibilities for grace, blessings and for the best outcome to work out for you. We have a limited capacity of what we can achieve in our life. Wayne Dyer said the best quote, "God laughs at our plans." We will sometimes be unplugged from the programs and systems that we are running to control our life. That element of control could be stopping you from where you need to be. If we are wanting a more spirit-filled life, then we have to be willing to surrender our desires and trust that they will be met beyond our limited capacity. Your inner guide knows exactly what you want. We have to break away from what we have been taught that brings us happiness and find our true inner bliss.

Every experience will lead you to where you need to be. As you shift through different experiences that can bring you a polarity of trauma or joy, these experiences are here to show you what needs to be shifted to live a life more in flow. Without these experiences, you wouldn't realise whether you need to leave that relationship or that job which makes you unhappy or that friendship that is really toxic for you. All paths will lead you to where you need to be, even if you are feeling that you are off track.

YOU WON'T KNOW UNTIL YOU LET GO

If you're holding onto a particular idea or want something to end up in a particular way, *it* could be stopping you from moving to *be* where you want to *be*. What we think is best for us can lead us into an experience that won't fulfil our soul and you may miss out on an opportunity that will expand your heart.

> **Stop trying to control an outcome that's not aligned with your soul.**
> **Let the Universe deliver for you.**

It's important for you to have dreams and for you to act on them. But if it compromises your ability to stay focused on your path, it won't transpire for you. Some dreams don't work because it's not meant for you and you've caught onto someone else's. This is why it's so important to learn to discover who you are, the beauty of your soul and what it really is asking for you in this lifetime to do. I know that I have been there. I've wanted something to turn out a certain way and I keep pushing up against a brick wall. Then I get frustrated but there's no-one to blame but myself because I was trying to do something that wasn't even a part of my path. I give up. Throwing my arms up in the air, having a few 'words' with the Universe and give up. Then hindsight later shows me that if I pursue that path it wouldn't have been truly fulfilling for me. I sigh and have a chuckle with the Universe and admit, *You were right!* I count the blessings that I have because I was actually in a better place than what I started when I was holding on to an idea or attachment that really wasn't good for me at all.

So, is there something within your heart which you know you need to release? Can you hear the Universe saying to you, "Please let go of this, we have got your back."

The power of surrender allows grace to enter our space but as long as you're holding onto what needs to leave, you are sabotaging the blessings which are awaiting to come through for you. Release the resistance to change or feeling the need to be in control, let the Universe take care of it for you. I know that you might just want to hold onto something for just a bit longer and keep doing the same things which you know you need to release. Open your mind and heart to the Universe and allow the infinite flow to work for you. As soon as you say, 'I surrender to a higher power to enact for the highest good of all, not my will but yours, allow me to shift to a higher perspective which will allow me to enact in a way which is congruent with my soul purpose,' breathe into that. Feel a power of peace and certainty flow through you and a weight lift off your shoulders. You are not blocked; you might just need to release the plughole so your blessings can come through. Your awareness is levelling up. Once you've obtained the courage to release that which you've clutched on dearly, you're able to develop an awareness of what needs to shift in your consciousness.

SOUL MASTERY INQUIRY

* What are you finding hard to let go of?
* What is leaving you now?
* How would your life be better if you chose to let it go?
* What do you need in order to completely let go and surrender?
* What is rising in you to act?

WHAT DO I NEED TO SHIFT?

As a soul, its wish is to expand. Feeling stuck can feel like torture. I know that I am someone who likes things to move quickly, it is one of the most painful experiences I can feel when it seems that nothing is happening. There's no inspiration. No clarity. It feels yuck! In this state, you have to ramp up the faith and show up more. If you feel uncomfortable, it means that your soul is growing, and you have to put the right procedures in place to receive your next transformation. It can feel really difficult and what is most important during this phase is that you never lose faith and stay true to your alignment. The alignment to your faith becomes your greatest blessing and strength.

Transitional times are testing periods of surrender where we are asked to become clearer about what we align to and how we spend our time and energy. Our focus becomes apparent that with whatever thought and action we choose to take that there is a purposeful intention behind it. When you are feeling stuck or stagnant, there's a part of your life that needs changing. This is so more flow can enter. You have to be strong enough to move through the transformation that is entering your life. When you are unclear about what you might need to change, start dissecting different parts of your life and ask spirit to give you the insight you need to. We are going to look at the dimensions for change that come under a few categories.

> Physical: health, fitness, nutrition, sleep, routines
> Environmental: home, nature
> Mental and Emotional: attitudes, thoughts, habits
> Relationships: partner, family, friends, peers, boundaries
> Life Purpose: career, travel, learning
> Spiritual: ritual, sacred, integration, expansion

PHYSICAL TRANSITIONS

Start with your physical layer first. Clean or change your house around. Your direct environment is a reflection on your mental state. Eat and drink cleaner. If you've been internal, go out and socialise. Clearing up your physical body and space allows for more clarity to come through for you. You may need to exercise to support yourself emotionally.

When we become lighter, we shed away the things that no longer serve as. We have to be careful because when we are going through some deep emotional trauma, we can use food to fill that hole of pain. It is a reason why, we may just need to be physical when we have no mental, emotional, relational, environmental factors to pinpoint. Movement generates energy. We say to the Universe we no longer want to be stuck and move forward with conviction.

Being physically active helps to shift through those deep emotions. When I've felt really sad and don't feel like doing or seeing anyone, I go to the gym and get really physical. I don't care even if I cry at the gym and look like a weirdo. I know that if I can make my physical body become stronger, I exert the emotional or mental fog that's clouding my space. I set an intention to get rid of as much as I can when I physically work out. I take the emotions outside of me and with every step or weights I push through, I push it out of me. Also, when our body feels and looks good, we can begin to feel good about ourselves. Use exercise as a processing time. It helps bring you back into the present where nothing else exists but complete perfection in that moment.

SOUL MASTERY INQUIRY

* Do you need more sleep?
* Do you feel sluggish or lacking energy?
* Do you crave quick-fix foods, yet really need good nourishing foods?
* Are you physically sick, more cold-like symptoms?
* Does your weight fluctuate?

ENVIRONMENTAL TRANSITIONS

As stated earlier, your environment reflects your internal state, or it can be a sign that you need to move or clear things up. I know that when I'm stressed or not making time for my soul, my immediate space is the first indicator that I can see where I need to make more time for myself. I always find that after I have taken some time to fix up my home or workplace, that I automatically start to feel better. It begins to translate straight away in my life as I can see immediate results in my productivity, an improvement in my relationships and I feel like I have more energy. Sometimes it only takes a spring clean to help change your feelings, mental state and spirit. Clean your room, give items to charity, open the blinds to get more light in, open your windows to move stagnant energy, change the layout of your house and workspace. Give love to every part of your environment. Bring nature inside by getting some nice plants. All these intentions help to bring more flow in your life.

Nature reminds us of the rhythmic cycles of life. Everything has a purpose, a cyclic process and works in seasons. Mother Earth has healing gifts to give you. Whether it's the oxygen you breathe, taking away the negative ions as you swim in the ocean or receiving the beautiful green healing ray through your eyes walking in a garden or forest. Nature reminds us to be present as it is a representative of the Earth's true form. Walk barefoot on the grass or sand and connect with the earth. Allow Gaia to support you as you walk through the transition on the physical layer of your being. Being in nature releases natural endorphins in your body. Be present with the sounds, senses and images around you and see how it can quickly get you back into that heart space.

Being in nature, changing your physical environment or being physical is a quick shift to change your overall wellbeing. Paying attention to the finer details of your environment may be exactly what the doctor ordered!

SOUL MASTERY INQUIRY

* Is your workspace or home neat and tidy?
* Do you feel an urge to do a spring clean?
* Do you go out in nature often?
* Do you need to improve the quality of your air?

MENTAL AND EMOTIONAL TRANSITIONS

Whatever actions we choose to make can be directly related to our mental or emotional state. When we are feeling low it could be because we haven't kept check on our mental state. What thoughts, habits or behaviours have been occurring? We have to sometimes come back to be the parent of our thought processes to redirect where we want energy to flow.

Our mental state is one of our greatest protectors for our energy. It is the conductor of what we allow to flow in our life. So, if our thoughts are from a fear or lack mentality, guess what you're going to experience? Exactly what you believe. As we deal with many processes, we can get stuck in blame, shame, fear or guilt. We might not even realise this is operating. The more we choose to think about these thoughts, it begins the downward spiral of our unconscious actions. Our mental state is what drives our actions. We act through 95% of our subconscious, the part of our being which are programmed from our thoughts. Our subconscious rules the daily actions we don't even think about. We don't even realise all the thoughts that are running through our mind. Or the little judgements we might be making. If you're overly emotional or being negative, it's time to retrain the subconscious to direct where you would like it to focus on and how you would like to feel and think.

The best way to start reprogramming our subconscious is to use powerful mantra statements accompanied with purposeful actions, such as, 'I AM'. You may need to listen to some inspirational talks whilst you are driving or working out. Any autonomous activity changes the brain waves, this is the perfect state where you can begin to retrain your brain to whatever you'd like it to be or think.

What feelings or thoughts would you like to experience each day? Stick with a process that works for you for at least 28 days. Each and every person has a different way in which they would like to program their brain. It might mean you may need a break from certain television shows, habits or people that influence your mindset. Catch your thoughts without judgement. It's only through realisation that transformation can occur. Without awareness, you don't have the capacity to change.

When you align your thoughts to your highest calling—even if you don't know what that is— the energy of the Universe has no choice but to flow in this space. It will begin to manifest in your world. You may wish to place some affirmations on sticky notes or paper around spaces where you will see them every day. Before you go to sleep, you may wish to write down five affirmations to reprogram your subconscious mind. Before you sleep and when you wake up are the perfect times to place these programs into the subconscious mind. As there has been no filters or distractions activated or setting off any negative patterns of thoughts or behaviours.

SOUL MASTERY INQUIRY

* Do negative thoughts creep in?
* Are you super emotional?
* Do you feel extra sensitive?
* Does your self-talk feel like someone else's?
* Do you look at life and think, *what's the point?*
* Are you unsure about your life's direction?

RELATIONSHIPS TRANSITIONS

Do you feel that your relationship with others, whether it is a lover or friendship, is changing? Have you outgrown your relationship? Have your feelings changed towards someone? Whether you are meant to say goodbye or work through it is why this transition period shows up for you. You are given this space to work through your subconscious patterns, ancestral patterns, unhealthy behaviours or habits that have served their time. It is important that when you are moving through the next phase of your life that it serves your highest good.

Unfortunately, we can get stuck in our own ways and not always able to see the things that are making us unhappy or stopping us from fulfilling our life purpose. If you're unsure whether it's the right time for you to let a certain person go, the Universe will show you and help you along the way. You will only ever be fully supported in making the decision that needs to be made.

Speak your truth. Be true to you and live authentically. Be aligned to your highest good, come from the space of love and have the capacity for forgiveness and compassion. It is only through this space can the decision whether to let them go or keep them around will be made. It's hard to stay connected with the people who knew you before your awakening if they are not somehow awakened themselves. Maybe you need a break from each other for a while.

The relationship will transcend. They either flow with you or flow away from you. Whether you are unwilling to make that challenging choice or finding it hard to know what's the right choice, you will be shown the way. Or out of nowhere they'll say that they can't have you in their life or there is movement in your environment. It is not easy. I had to let go of my best friend who helped me rise up so much, yet she was one of the most toxic people ever to be in my life. She acted as my catalyst for my greatest awakening. For that I'm grateful. Everyone who enters our life will be here to remind us of our path and what lessons we need to move through to grow as a soul. To move on, see the gifts that they bring in your relationship. This can be seen through the challenges that they bring. Do they push you into your power? Are you needing to be a pillar of light or love, unfazed with what's thrown at you?

SOUL MASTERY INQUIRY

* Do you feel disconnected to someone more than usual?
* Do conversations on a superficial level no longer serve you?
* Do you want to avoid toxic people or certain circumstances that feel negative more often?
* Do you feel your worst Self comes out when you're around certain people?

LIFE PURPOSE TRANSITIONS

As soon as you are awakened you become aware that there is something that you need to do in this lifetime. More than what you are doing now. From birth you have already been aligned to your purpose. This transition can take a while until you see it transpire. You may already be doing what you love and that's great. Once your awake, guilt can creep in that maybe you've been wasting your time, but I can assure you that you have been initiated at the right time. Your awakening couldn't have happened at any other time, only now. If you hadn't experienced life as an illusion, then you wouldn't have had the capacity to connect with the people around you to develop the insights you need for this next phase of your life.

Finding out who you are gives you the greatest insights on what you're meant to do in life. The best thing you can do for yourself is to continue to work out who you are and do what lights you up. It might mean you're meant to be in the same line of work with a new enlightened awareness to help those around you. When you're in the phase of not knowing what your purpose is, bring in what you love and your best Self in every place you go. Here, you allow your divine Self to unfold in an environment that may be looking for hope, light and transformation. At times, challenges and difficulties may come your way. This sometimes acts as a confirmation that you are needing to move on. The door might appear, it's your choice to walk through it.

You don't find your purpose; your purpose finds you.

Letting go of the constructs of how you perceive you purpose to be and the expectations that comes along with that, will have to be released as this may stop you from moving forward to where you need to be. I understand how frustrating it can feel, on an intellectual level, you can feel your soul knowing your next step and for you to be somewhere else and you don't know where and what that is.

**Soul time is quicker than our Earth time.
Be patient.
Patience will always be rewarded.**

There are moments where we may be in a void period. During this period, ask for assistance to be in a place that is supportive to your life purpose and keeps you lit up. I've been in places where I have to work hard to keep that light shining through. It's not always easy when we know that during any transition phase, it's uncomfortable. Continue to show up where your heart expands the most. No matter how odd it might be. The path of the soul is illogical, but it will show you the quickest way to your fulfillment.

> ## SOUL MASTERY INQUIRY
> * Are you confused what your soul purpose is?
> * Do you often want to give up on life?
> * Do you feel like the Universe isn't supporting you?
> * Does your work feel unfulfilling?
> * Does it feel like everywhere you turn in your workplace there is a block, or it feels out of flow, this can be the Universe showing you that it's time to make that tough choice and move on.

SPIRITUAL TRANSITIONS

Has your spiritual practice faltered, or does something need to be altered? You have to enjoy what you do. I've never been a yoga fan, but I love to meditate. If you have cut down on your meditation, increase it. If you're meditating a lot, maybe add something else to the mix. Are you sacrificing others needs before your own or have some actions that you've taken aren't inspiring for your being?

Every transition period is a time of alignment.

As hard as it can be, on another level you are preparing yourself for the next stages for your soul's growth. Your soul growth asks you to up your spiritual practice. This is anything that brings you back into your spirited Self. Whatever that is for you, do it. Bring the routine for your sacred Self to emerge each day. As you are lifting your vibration, you'll have to give time to release any energetic debris and give time to increase your light quotient.

There are times that the only way the Universe can get to us is by stopping our physical body, so we pay attention to something that's pivotal for our expansion. Sometimes you may get a cold or flu that knocks you out for a few days. As soon as I have the onset of any form of strain, I know that I'm needing to pay attention to something. It might be my thoughts, an opportunity to recharge, to have a synchronistic opportunity or change an element of my life that I might not have been conscious of. As energy creators, as we enter any space, I know how hard it is to just sit and be when all we want to do is keep moving forward.

Spiritual transitions can be one of the hardest to navigate as we come back to the questions: Who am I? What is my purpose here? What am I meant to do with my life?

What served you in the past, may no longer serve you now and this just shows the growth you've accomplished. Be proud of your achievements and how far you've come. During this transitional period, we may be faced with owning our own *stuff*. We can feel the need to be serious, as the stuff that has been locked up in the closet comes out, we actually have to ramp up the joy. Even if joy is the furthest emotion you want to feel in that moment. Know that you're worthy to feel good along the way. We aren't meant to live the path of suffering. I don't believe that suffering is what we are called to do.

It's during this period we have to find the joy and magic of life again. The true essence of the Divine. To rekindle that spark with the Divine. When we rediscover that which is majestic, we can tap back into life again. We can't see this in the lens of seriousness. It is only through the lens of a childlike curiosity of the world can we begin to open a spiritual perspective of the world. Here, we rediscover our magic and flow again.

SOUL MASTERY INQUIRY

* Do you feel out of flow?
* Do you feel like you're alone and no-one understands you?
* Do you feel out of routine in your spiritual practice?
* Does your guidance feel unclear?
* Are you super emotional, have weight fluctuations?
* Do you isolate yourself from the world?
* Are you lacking joy?
* Do you have Cold/Flu like symptoms often?

Any transition we go through is a sign that our focus has to come back to the present moment. To reflect on where your life is heading and what you need to do right now. This is the most powerful energy generator for momentum. Shifting back to the now can help accelerate your transition periods. If you are busy drowning in the transition by becoming a victim of it without constructive change, you run the risk of having pity on yourself. Then the domino affect occurs. Our attention turns to the healing steps we are going to take to move through whatever you feel is happening to you. Transitions are helping you to up level into a better vibe and frequency which helps to ultimately transform your life. They are a sign that you're ready for a breakthrough so don't give up!

ACCESSING HIGHER GUIDANCE

It's through taking time to reflect that we can access our subconscious mind. A gateway to the insights of our Higher Self. It's here that, if your intention is set in gaining the highest wisdom, you can receive the divine guidance, as your highest guidance is an extension of Source.

Writing activates the empathetic part of our brain that helps us move from our logical mind to the right hemisphere. It helps to access both parts and acts as a bridge between your ego Self and your divine Self. When you write you're able to distinguish between what's coming from your true Self, and what's coming from your lower Self. Reflection helps to shift the momentum of stagnant energy and helps to reignite the flow of what you truly want to put your energy into.

When you recognise that which isn't in alignment and acknowledge it allows your soul presence to penetrate through. As the light will always illuminate that which is not congruent with your Highest Self. You'll always be pulled to solitude when there's something that needs transcending.

PAY ATTENTION TO THE SIGNS.

YOUR SOUL IS CALLING YOU.

HEALING

You will be attracted to what is perfect for your soul to heal. There's no right or wrong or better healing modality. I had a client rock up to a Crystal Bed session saying she didn't believe in it and only believed in Reiki. Therefore, she came in with an idea about what she believed would help her. My ego felt conflicted that she would come to a healing session that is totally against what she wanted. My heart knew that we can never close ourselves to healing and learning which can happen in any moment. As a practitioner, it's my job to hold a sacred space and act as a pure channel. All I did was hold space for her. Boy, did she get an awakening from that session!

Everyone we meet and the circumstances which occur in our life is a divine assignment. Each person gives us an opportunity to learn a lesson. They are a divine messenger here to support your life purpose—even when it doesn't feel that way with certain people—the same can be said with everything that we experience. It's hard to know the exact plan of our life and every single detail, as if we knew everything, I'm sure that life would become boring. We receive what we need to know.

We can also get addicted to healings, healers and particular spiritual leaders. Don't get stuck in attachment. Do what is right for your soul but don't become dependent on finding answers outside of you. When life is happening to you outwardly, it means we need to go inwardly. Anything that makes you become addicted to seeking the answers outwardly is what you will need to break away from. We all have a shaman, or healer or a great friend we turn to for support and it's important that we seek support when we are in a funk. True healing occurs when you understand that *they* act as a catalyst for your change—rather than them taking responsibility for your change—you heal yourself. When you go for a healing, you're taking time out to show up to the Universe and allowing someone to hold that space for you. I know that when I've sought desperately for answers outside of myself, I get the complete opposite. Every time a circumstance is occurring for you in your life, it provides an opportunity for you to strengthen your faith in the Universe. Allow the Universal Healing Agency to work for you. They always are hearing and responding to your every call and every conscious intention you put out there.

Difficulties are an opportunity for your soul to grow and it accelerates your evolution process. As long as you're willing to transcend the thoughts and feelings to a higher perspective, you are growing as a soul.

We may receive the same lessons in this lifetime, but your comeback rate to your heart space can become quicker, and the same things that may have affected you in the past, affect you with less intensity and for a shorter healing duration. It is during this period of time that you are being either asked to go back to the basics or find another avenue to heal. This may open new opportunities for your path and helps to recalibrate every cell in your body to respond to the call you're giving out to the Universe. It might be going to a meditation or yoga class, a fitness class or a social event because it means that you're meant to meet or experience something that's so integral to your path. Every feeling, thought, or physical ailment all have a message. Our physical body and senses act as a feedback mechanism. We have to dig deeper to find out the answers. I know that every time I have been sick, it's meant I've been doing too much. I haven't been honouring myself, or I've needed some writing time as there are some important messages to channel through.

SOUL MASTERY INQUIRY

If you're not feeling your full 100% energy—mind, body and spirit—close your eyes, breathe and ask yourself:

* What part of me do I need to honour right now?
* What message of wisdom does this ailment impart?
* How does this (whatever is troubling you) help me and my soul growth?
* What is one action step that I can take this week to make myself feel better?
* How can I incorporate more love to my body, mind, relationships and work?

Ask empowering questions and the Universe will respond with the answers you need. If you ask the Universe, *why am I sick?* Then you could receive a negative answer rather than using your insight to see the wisdom and blessings of what everything brings you. The answer to your healing always comes back to love. Giving and receiving more love. In love there is perfect equilibrium and balance. No judgements about what might be troubling you. It just is. This is all in Divine order. Love and peace vibrate higher in frequency. Breathe to shift the momentum of any lower thought forms or feelings.

The test of your healing journey comes down to faith. Many people pilgrimage all over the world to receive healing. Your healing is both you and the Universe showing up. Many people record miraculous healings. Believe in the power of miracles.

You will only receive what you are completely capable of. For some, an illness that presents in their life may not be able to shift. Or an unimaginable circumstance might occur. This is because that 'illness' is not meant to be healed or that challenging event needed to occur because it is part of the Soul Blueprint. There is a great gift that the soul has chosen to give to this world through their hardship. It can feel really unfair if this has happened to you. We either become a victim of circumstance and let our stories dictate our future, or we empower our whole being and use the hardship for the greatest good of all. Your suffering offers an opportunity to connect with others who might've gone through the same things as you. It might inspire you to create a specialised group, create an organisation to help stop and fight whatever happened to you. Whatever it is for you or that person, the transcendence of suffering is peace. You are worthy of peace and contentment in your heart and life. You are the director of your life. The story of your suffering can change from that of pain to peace. How you choose to end it is entirely up to you. Some days can feel easier than others. I'm not saying that whatever is happening is okay, but if there's a lack of acceptance then there's resentment and toxic emotions that can also sever your connection and trust in the Universe. The Universe is always supporting you and your growth, leading you to the path of love, support and peace.

SOUL MASTERY LESSON

* Trust whatever healing modality is right for you. There's no wrong choice.
* Choose what resonates with your soul.
* Allow someone to hold you a sacred space if it's too intense for you.
* Someone will be there whenever you need help.
* What you experience is perfectly orchestrated from your Soul Blueprint.
* Every person you interact with is a divine assignment designed for your soul's evolution in some shape or form.
* Find what keeps you in balance and stick with it.

A SACRED PRACTICE

The ancients have left us clues on how to live a fulfilled life. After all, they did have a strong connection with the Divine. Life was determined by the flow of nature. Ritual brought about culture, a sense of the Divine working within and outside themselves. This brought about miracles, peace and connection. Something that many of us miss today. Being consumed by being busy, we miss the blessings that are bestowed upon us each day and instead we tend to feel out of flow. Rituals invoke an ancient aspect of our being that invites presence, love and peace. When we are ruled by time, we can neglect the blessings of our ancestors and how the Divine works through us. Our eyes can't be open to the Divine at work if we don't allow this presence to be visible. Rituals connect and tap us back into flow.

Developing a spiritual practice or ritual helps to ensure a sense of sacredness within oneself and really helps when we are going through a deep spiritual transition. I don't enjoy transition periods, as I can be impatient, and I want things to happen now. But circumstances funnily enough work out perfectly when we surrender, then surrender some more. What I find magical is that we begin to tap into synchronicity. Even when we are in a transition period, we are still in synchronicity.

We just can't see the rewards, but the Universe will always reward a believer. However, to ensure that we are staying in a state of alignment and purpose we need to ensure that we are creating moments for our soul.

How can we have those sacred moments in our busy modern world? Your sacred practice can include running a bubble bath, meditating, going for a walk, lighting a candle, sipping that cup of coffee, whatever it is for you invite and invoke your soul to come in. Get to know and love being in your presence. This is how your intuition gets stronger, guidance becomes clearer and we allow space to experience our soul. If you get bored with your sacred practice, mix it up. The more you become committed to your path, the more you will be guided to find ways in which you feel more at home, in your spirit, which can only happen when you allow time for your ritual to happen.

This way you become one heartbeat and frequency with the universe and can tap into your soul much more easily. You can also use rituals to help you move through any soul theme you might be going through. Maybe you need to let go of that relationship, job or an addition that has been driving you crazy! Rituals are like initiations and invite new beginnings and new chances in the present moment. You are a beautiful soul. It is time to honour you and all those working for you in spirit, through a sacred practice.

SOUL MASTERY INQUIRY

* When is the best time to commit to your ritual? Daily? Monthly?
* What ritual or practice gets you back feeling at home with your soul?

* What have you tried in the past that isn't working for you now?
* What are you willing to try now to include in your rituals?

WHEN YOU TAKE THAT STEP OF FAITH, YOU TAKE THAT STEP INTO SYNCHRONISTICAL FLOW.

THE VOID

There are times when we may feel there's no motion and it can feel frustrating because all you want to do is move forward, but you have no clarity or momentum. It is in these moments that we are being asked to have faith and surrender to the unknown. The theme of transition periods is that word surrender again! Even when we feel nothing is happening, the Universe is moving mountains and the entire galaxy for you. There are important lessons needing time to illuminate. As frustrating as feeling that you're in a period of time where all you might want is clarity and it's not happening, you have to stay true to your alignment and trust the process that it's all working in your favour.

During this transitional phase, the void is a clear sign that what you need to change is going to become illuminated. It's through the moments where you're not sure where to direct your presence and energy that you're given an opportunity to see what it is that will help you along your path. You are at a threshold, the place for deep soul revelation so that you can move forward. Your revelation is coming and so is your quest for transformation. The revelation comes from what needs to transform from fear into love, so that the presence of your soul can come through for you more deeply. The presence of the heart can't be heard through the noise of the world; therefore, the void activates stillness so that whatever is holding you back from living the life you desire can be made clear.

THE MISSING YEARS

Being immersed into the process world for so long can make you feel that you're really stuck in a bottomless pit. You judge feeling any sense of elation knowing that possibly you did something or didn't do enough in this lifetime or another. The more I kept digging and the deeper I went the harder it was to get out of the cycle of emotions.

You may feel this even for yourself. Where has the time gone? Your intense emotions have felt like they've sucked the life out of you. There comes a point where you just have to stop digging and start living. I was so committed to clearing my crap that I missed out on the joy of life. The process of constantly unfolding who you are becomes entangled within and you actually have no idea who you are. How do you get out of this? Your processes that were meant to release judgement can creep into more judgement on the Self and on others. Self-attack is the worst kind of attack you can make. I can be great at it. We are told that we can justify our feelings towards someone or a circumstance and instead of releasing this we go deeper so it sticks with us. Like sticky tar surrounding our body, we have to spend some time undoing the conditioning that we might not be aware on the subconscious level. The ambiguity, the lack of clarity can come when we have gone too deep and we need to resurface to get some air. Take a deep breath.

During the missing years—which lasted about three years where I can't recall where time went—the intense polarities of my emotions existed. In my deep processes I knew I was transcending lifetimes of pain, suffering and karma. I knew I needed to shift it coming into this lifetime. Coming out of it, I felt I was stuck more in pain than joy. I couldn't understand why I wasn't transcending the lessons. Joy generates energy and momentum and I was finding it hard to connect into it. It helps to lift a layer of anything that might be stuck in your auric layer that has been hard to shift. The important part of life is to stay connected with Spirit. I had lost my Spirit and my connection to Spirit or found it in only fleeting moments. It's actually hard to write about without feeling some sort of emotion about it. I resented Spirit for a while because I had 'done the work' and where did it lead me? To more disappointment and sadness.

I began to not believe in the magic of life anymore. I looked back in time wondering where did my spark go? Maybe that I was a fool along this path and the Gods were punishing me from every transgression, every thought I had and every action. I had self-judgement because some beliefs were that I was creating this reality, and this made me hate myself even more. The Universe that I believed was all good was showing me constantly what I needed to 'work on' because I was preaching good but maybe this wasn't the truest reflection of myself. I'd never felt so alone. I felt abandoned by everyone in life, including Spirit. It was like being in Hell with myself. This perception is only an illusion, of course. An illusion that was running my reality. It was like being stuck in Jumanji, unable to get out of the game until I worked on everything that was wrong with me. I was also disheartened by people in the religious or spiritual industry. People I looked up to, preaching love demonstrated the complete opposite. I began to disown the associated parts of me that made up my spirited Self because I had been hurt by so many people I had idolised.

Never put anyone on a pedestal. This opened my eyes to the illusion that we place on people. It also increased my BS meter and I wasn't up for falling into an infatuation. I was already feeling let down. There are people that I know who are well known in the spiritual industry that have high followers and I couldn't believe that what they preached, isn't what was executed. Then it came back to me questioning, *how do these people get into these positions?* Everyone is playing out the journey they're meant to. I was questioning Spirit's integrity, rather than understanding the divine plan at play. A spiritual persona is not authentic. You being you is. The blessing of this was that I learnt how to look to Spirit for answers, rather than others. Finding the answers within. Even when I felt the most disconnected, I always asked Spirit for signs to assist me. They always came through.

I didn't realise how much I was mistrusting Spirit as I was looking for instances where I could disbelieve what I know is true. I had to mend my relationship with Source, life and the people who let me down in life. Philosophies, spiritual leaders and practices are like trying on clothes. Some will be a great fit for you, others won't and over time it might be that you have to chuck out a piece because it's either out of season or doesn't fit you anymore. I got lost in other identities. Even when it comes to inspirational speakers, they are all human. Take the practice that serves you. But never belittle yourself. You may find that you lose yourself idolising someone until Spirit brings you back to earth to show you that no-one is better or less than you. Keep empowered and stay true to you. Losing yourself in someone or an external identity is the same as losing yourself in a relationship.

My hope is that you don't experience the void of missing out on life because you're stuck on processes because life makes you confront your stuff. We are sometimes told to face something in the mirror, it's not meant to act as self-judgement, but how many of you do that? I'm not sure what your mind is like, but mine can be a monkey mind. Anything that isn't acted in integrity I go in a negative self-attack ninja mode. In this mode, whatever positive aspect someone says to me, I can't accept because the veil of emotions clouds my ability to see the good in me.

Spirit doesn't want us to stay stuck. Spirit wants us to move through things so that we can live a self-actualised life. If you lose faith in the Universe, you lose faith in life. There are important parts in your Soul Blueprint that need to be accomplished. Although you are evolving as a soul, know who you are inside. Come back to what brings you joy. Joy is an expression from within, a lightness of heart.

Being stuck in your emotions dampens your spark for life, but it never stops it from shining. If you're stuck in the processes for too long, you will begin to believe that this is your current reality. Your current reality affects your physical, emotional and mental state. You weren't made to stay stuck, rather to transcend your suffering by not staying in it. Our Spirit is continuous. Remember, that for a habit to change, it takes about 28 days. Imagine that if every day you are stuck reflecting, deep within emotions having judgmental thoughts, this will affect your perception on your reality. This happened to me for over three years. Until I had enough of scrubbing clean. I was done with the deep processes and feeling fleeting moments of joy instead of more positive emotions.

You might feel done too. Now is the time to create change.

How can you come back to life now when you've been submerged for so long? A childlike nature is what can help bring back that purity in our life. Laughter, joy, curiosity, innocence, fun, socializing, care-free, these are the keys to help us generate a lighter heart. When you feel you've missed the boat of life, jump on the ship of the innocence of a child. Play with life. You forget that your true nature is of a Divine Creator. If you feel that you've lost your connection, reconnect back with Spirit through finding joy again and trust in the process. Whatever you align to becomes your reality.

Say,

I forgive myself for everything I have or have not done.

I forgive Spirit and ask to be forgiven for judging myself, life, and placing expectations on you when you were guiding me all along to live my life fully.

I ask for my connection with Spirit to be reignited and my intuition strengthened.

I ask to be fully aligned with Soul Blueprint and execute that with conviction and courage. I fulfil it with ease and grace.

I ask that each step gets revealed to me.

Please allow the grace of the Divine to enter every aspect of my being and my life so that the veil of illusion that separates me from the Divine becomes lifted.

May unconditional love filter through every part of my life.

Please fill me with the courage, power and wisdom to fulfil my purpose and lift me out of anything that clouds my ability to connect and flow with life.

Bless me and protect me.

Allow me to integrate with a light heart any processes that need be discovered and shifted.

I ask for a higher perspective to shine through for me.

Allow a shower of light to penetrate through all layers of my auric field so that all I can feel in the true nature of the Divine.

May the gift of life be present in my life and may my presence become fully actualised.

May your *divine presence* be so great that it places beyond doubt the miracles and gifts that you bring to life.

Please continue to help me become my Divine Self.

And so it is.

SOUL MASTERY VISUALISATION

When you close your eyes, see that beautiful spark within your heart burning and shining bright. This is always guiding you. Your Spirit team is connected to this inner light. Call upon the Council of Light to guide you and intervene to work your divine Soul Blueprint. Ask any layers of your being that's holding onto anything that is holding you back to let go. Breathe. Allow a bright light to flow through every cell in your body. Rejuvenated and restored on all levels.

SOUL MASTERY LESSON

* If you're in the void, stay true to your alignment.
* Trust that a deep soul revelation is coming to you when you least expect it.
* You're on the threshold of your breakthrough. Be still.

THE UNIVERSE IS WORKING FOR YOU

Whether you can see progress or not, there is a Universal force that is working behind the scenes for you. During transitional phases, magic is happening without you even knowing. We can feel as if our prayers aren't being heard, but I assure you, they are opening all the doors for you so that you *can* live a life that will bring about true heart fulfilment. A part of us needs to relinquish how we think life should be controlled and allow the universe to do what it does best.

Spirit knows what's really best for you and it's helping you to see that too. But we have to let go of our control and resisting the change that needs to happen because if we are doing this, we are choosing to stay stuck. Release that need for your order and allow a divine order to work for you because if you're continuously asking for help and keep doing actions that don't support helping you, then you're prolonging the process for your blessings to come through for you.

You might *think* you know what's best, but Spirit knows the truth of what's best for your heart and path. Don't worry, the Universe will never give up on you and they will continue to move all the obstacles in your path, until you see the light which has been awaiting you this whole time.

SOUL MASTERY INQUIRY

* Is there something you might need to relinquish control over?
* What signs is the Universe showing you right now that shows that it is working for you with your life path and alignment?

TRANSITION SUMMARY

Transitions take time because they are leading you to your alignment and purpose. Time is needed to ensure that your alignment is filtered through all levels of your being to every thought, atom and particle. During transitional phases, you obtain a deeper awareness on what needs to shift, begin to obtain the resources you need in order to change and get into a powerful alignment with your soul.

Once you become all in with your alignment, it's as if the momentum to move forward is met with a powerful force. You can feel this rush of energy surge through you. It's like everything feels as if it's finally clicking into place. It is then that you know that you are ready. Your authentic Self can finally begin to express itself naturally. Transitional periods can feel hard because you're on the threshold of a breakthrough. You can feel frustrated because you are neither here nor there, but you know on a deep level that something is stirring within. It might not be completely evident yet but when it does come through, you can feel this miraculous infinite force work through you.

Your preparation now becomes complete to change and integrate into your new soul alignment. Be prepared to do the work. This is a time to get acquainted with your soul. Meditate, trust your intuition and stay true in your heart what your intended desires are.

SOUL MASTERY LESSON

* Don't panic. This is a time to clear out the junk in your life.
* Keep doing the work.
* If it gets too hard, ask for a Higher Power to assist you or give you a break for a few days to integrate all the changes.
* Keep up your spiritual practice.
* Change your routine.
* You are becoming stronger in your alignment into what will fulfil your heart and soul.
* See the blessing that you're releasing all the stuff that's stopping you receiving what would truly give you joy. So, let it go!

AND FINALLY, DON'T GIVE UP! YOU'VE GOT THIS!

PART IV
CHANGE AND INTEGRATION

Attract change and allow time for integration to occur

*Yesterday I was clever, so I wanted to change the world.
Today I am wise, so I am changing myself.*

— RUMI

SOUL ALIGNMENT

Without proper integration, change cannot happen and vice versa. Changing who you are becomes imperative and intertwined as a necessary process to ensure that your thoughts, actions and any momentum you create comes in full alignment to where you're guided as a soul. If you change without a proper integration, you may be tempted to go back to your old ways, attachments and identity (the one that kept you in suffering and stay bound). Commitment to your change is a marathon but once the old behaviour, habits and attitudes is transcended this is when you can truly begin to feel and create a new soulfully nourished life.

You must give space and time to transcend to a new way.

Once you make that acknowledgement and accept of what it is that needs to change, it's almost as if all the stars align and a force comes whooshing through like a fast-paced train that you have no control over how you get to the destination, only knowing that you'll get there along the ride. It is the alignment that powerfully integrates your soul. You've been wanting this. Calling this on a conscious or unconscious level. It needed to happen.

GETTING IN SYNC

Yes! Finally, it feels that everything is coming into place. The joy after the chaos. The signs that you're coming out of a transitional phase becomes evident when you begin to feel a shift in your consciousness and overall awareness of your mind and body. It is as if you have become 'in-sync' with a universal flow and it's beginning to look like a divine order has taken over. When you are in this state it feels as if everything is just going your way. You attract events, people, circumstances, abundance and experiences that can't be explained. I wish I could say once you're here that you'll stay here. People and circumstances will show up and you will experience divine grace flow through your being. But, how can you tap into the magic of synchronicity and stay in flow? Go where there is flow. It's easy to let go of your spirited practice during this state—keep it up! Savour each and every moment. Place them into your cellular memory as important events in your life, because if you feel like you're in a funk, anchoring these memories helps to change your state and energy. Big synchronistical events remind us of the magic this Universe holds.

Enjoy the moments where you feel magic and elated joy. Don't feel it can't last because it can. It can feel too good to be true, but don't let your thoughts creep in to make you believe in a reality where you can't experience good things in your life. In this state of flow, decisions are acted upon with clarity and conviction—without any questions—even if it appears strange to the mind. For me, I find my greatest synchronistical flow is when I travel overseas. Habits and old routines have no place in a new environment. Like a child, you're open with unlimited possibilities. In 2015, I went to America, there were many synchronistical events that took place that could be seen as coincidence but in this synergetic state, you can't question that a greater presence is taking over. I booked long service leave to go and celebrate my thirtieth birthday. In a school system in Australia, you need to book a year in advance, depending on your employer. When I set my intention to have this time off, I didn't know how it would play out. A few months leading up to my birthday, I noticed that Gabby Bernstein was holding her annual *Spirit Junkie* Masterclass in New York. I was to finish work that same Friday it was on, so I tried to find flights that could possibly get me there in time. No matter how hard I looked, it didn't seem feasible, so I let that idea go and thought I'd just go to Maui and attend the Hay House, *Writing From Your Soul* workshop.

> **When you need to be somewhere and do something, the magic of the Universe will always come through. Serendipity.**

A few months before *Spirit Junkie* Masterclass, I looked at my work calendar. I noticed that it was a student free day on that Friday for a report writing day. *This couldn't be?* It meant that I had the possibility to go to New York, after all, and make it in time. When I looked at booking the tickets, the plane was to arrive at JFK airport at 6 p.m. *Spirit Junkie* Masterclass was at 7:30 p.m. I wasn't sure if I was able to make it, but I just prayed and meditated hard. I thought if I missed the night session, at least I had another two days to make this possible. I got into the airport at 6 p.m. Miraculously, my bags were one of the first to collect in baggage, so I hardly spent any time at the airport. I could make it! My sister had organised a cab for me, so I even had a ride ready to go. I got to my hotel at 7 p.m. I'd booked around the corner from the venue. I had time to quickly shower, get ready. I arrived to the *Spirit Junkie* Masterclass right on time. This trip continued to flow on. I met some amazing people, explored the city of dreams and had never felt my heart so open. I felt alive. In synchronistical flow, this is all you feel.

You wouldn't know from the above story, but I had to completely let go of my home world where I was experiencing some extremely difficult circumstances. I felt in two worlds. I had to let go of my world because it was hard for me to fly when there were people trying to hold me down. I mention this because even when we are in flow, we can still experience some intense pain, but the flow doesn't stop. Continue with your momentum because it's important for your soul's evolution. Don't get sucked into the cycle that gets you stuck in something you don't want to be in. It takes courage to live in synchronicity because your actions are illogical to someone who is coming from another perspective.

After the *Spirit Junkie* Masterclass weekend, I headed to Maui, Hawaii, to attend the *Writing From Your Soul* workshop with Dr Wayne Dyer and Doreen Virtue. I sat on the beach chanting abundance mantras every day and recharging in the sun. The day before the workshop, I was running along Ka'anapali Beach and I had this thought: *If I'm meant to write a book, I'll see Wayne Dyer or Doreen Virtue today. Just kidding, Universe.*

Because I didn't want to make the Universe feel that I was putting them to the test, I figured that was my ego speaking. After that, I saw a Starbucks along the way so decided to stop and get some water. I sat down and, in that moment, who did I see run into Starbucks? Dr Wayne Dyer. If anyone was watching me from a distance, they would have seen my jaw drop and my colour turn a ghostly white. I couldn't believe it! He ran out and I ran behind him for about ten minutes along the beach. I wanted to go up to him but decided to respect his space as he was on the phone. *Wow! Thanks Universe. Message received.* If the timing was right, I knew I'd get another opportunity to meet him again. The next day, that's exactly what happened.

Whenever someone asks me to tell them about Maui, I'm taken back to that sequence of events: Starbucks, the beach, that feeling. It makes my whole being melt and my heart expand. It's important to remember these core important events that happen in our life. As our life occurs simultaneously, we can access the gateway of universal flow when we remember an event that expanded us. Don't think of it as a distant memory. The power of the mind is that even in its 'imagined' state, we can feel and experience the same moment we did in the past, in the present. Do you also remember how in your awakened state you saw all those signs but didn't know what it all meant? In a synchronistic state, you may begin to see amped up all those number sequences, coins, strange and bizarre coincidences that now all begin to make sense. This is the synchronistic state of be-ing. You're on the right track!

SOUL MASTERY LESSON

* Keep up your spiritual routine.
* Keep up your positive self-talk.
* Stay aligned to your authentic truth and Higher Self.

- Act in what is in accordance with what feels right for you.
- Do flowy activities.
- Breathe and be conscious.
- Acknowledge and thank the signs that you continue to receive.

BREAKING CO-DEPENDENCY

I admit, I have been a psychic-reading-healing-junkie. Even when my intuition was prophetic, I would still seek the answers externally. When I had psychics make predictions that I knew in my heart and soul were *not* true, I still doubted my own ability. I found out the hard way. For me, I'm so passionate about empowering others to find the answers from their own inner guide. I am happy to act as a guide which can be frustrating because we are an instant feedback society. However, if you have the patience, determination and commitment to Spirit, then you will learn how you can tap into more flow with the Universe.

I received a big slap from the Universe when I wasn't listening and refused to see the signs they were constantly sending me. I kept choosing to believe what someone else would *see* my future for me. Without this lesson I wouldn't be here where I am today. I was in an abusive relationship. It brought me more pain than joy. I needed to go and have a 'healing' nearly every week because I had so much emotional abuse. Every time I would go and see this healer they would say things to me like, 'This person is your twin flame, the one you're meant to spend the rest of your life with,' or, 'Whether you like it or not, you will end up with this person, even if you leave them.' This under no circumstances is healthy or helpful for someone who is emotionally vulnerable.

For a long time, I believed this was true and every week I was distraught. When I left my partner, I felt ashamed and guilty that I was letting go of 'the one'. It was only after my experience when I went to John of God that I truly opened my eyes to the illusion that I was shown. Spirit was showing me so many signs along the way that it wasn't healthy, but I wasn't willing to believe what I knew was true for me. For me, this was a turning point. I knew I wanted to help others who were stuck in the illusion of 'the Guru' and empower people to make spirit filled choices. To stick to the truth of their being and not the intentions of others. After all, we are the driver along this journey making choices in which direction to go. Some will lead you where you need to go, others may lead to a dead end. You can't continue driving at a dead end. There has to be a time when you have to make the choice to take a U-turn, go back and keep driving along another road. The road you know was the right way all along.

Are you becoming your self-actualised Self or embodying someone else's identity? Are your thoughts your own or do they reflect the guru you idolize?

Allow the truth of your soul to be your authentic voice. By doing so, you strengthen your connection to the Universe and act on your Soul Blueprint instead of trying to live a life of someone else's mission. Some of the truths they speak might ring true in your being, but still, at the end of a sermon, come back into your own Self. Ask yourself, does this—whatever guidance or wisdom they have imparted—serve me, inspire me and reflect my soul essence? If it's a no, you know what to do.

THE SPIRITUAL EGO

As we continue to grow on our spiritual journey, we will gain knowledge on many spiritual concepts that will in turn be our truth. Nevertheless, I believe some perceptions of the spiritual industry has it wrong. It's not what you know but what you experience that's pivotal in experiencing the Divine in every moment. Attaining knowledge is important but applying it and experiencing it is what makes all the difference.

I've studied a lot of crazy things. Earlier on in my journey I wanted to show people what I knew, so I spoke spiritual jargon to them so that they wouldn't question what I was doing. Part of my personality wanted to be validated for all the work I had done. I tried hard to earn the respect of people who were in the industry. A few times, I'd tell them what I knew and was doing. Deep down my ego wanted to be heard and validated. *Look at me and what I know!* The irony is, when you're doing 'the work' in full flow, you don't need to do anything. You will be seen, heard, validated and felt because people will feel the radiance of your soul.

We want people to join us along the journey to help them to transform their lives as deep within our being we feel the call to help everyone. Often, we displace our beliefs as we try to make *them* merge with our beliefs, because we are excited about the transformation that's taking place. It is going to sound simple, but all you need to do if you are really wanting to help people on their journey is to just be yourself. The best version of yourself. This is a continuous journey. When we live our life from this space, it raises our vibration to another level and the Universe has no choice but to match that frequency.

You will be guided towards a mentor and may even become one. The moment you feel like a teacher is when your students will appear, and you will become another student of life. If a guru says, 'You need to stay with me your whole life to attain a certain spiritual level.' That's disempowerment. You can learn their teachings, see what feels right for you, your soul. Our true teacher will always be the Universe and what it presents to us each and every day. The Universe is a true teacher as it knows how to challenge, grow and give us exactly what we can handle.

Inspiration always gives us a clue that we are touching an aspect of our essence. The moment we begin to act out in a spiritualist ego, we lose our integrity around people we love. Instead of inspiring them to be their best Self, in that moment, they are repulsed by our actions. Who could blame them? So, stay in your integrity and trust your feelings or a big lesson will be headed your way.

Another play by the spiritual ego is where you rate your 'vibration' in accordance with someone else's journey. This is judgement. No-one is keeping tabs on you. No-one is recording your level of frequency. Don't have tickets on yourself. The Universe doesn't look at you and say, 'I like you better than that person because you have a higher vibration.' If you truly want to be the Light, you'll have to get your hands dirty and this can't be attained by secluding yourself on a mountain forever. There are people who may be stuck in negative thoughts and this is a lower density, but they are still human. As human beings, we are vibrating at a lower density. We are made up of matter. That's how we exist. You can choose to become lighter through your thoughts, feelings and actions. You can feel it, but when you place yourself on a high vibrational pedestal, this is a lower vibrational judgement. Excluding yourself and judgement can be seen as an action of fear, not love. When you are in the space of someone who you feel may drain your energy, there is a secret that's at play. Hold strong in your pillar of light and people will match this vibration, the law of the Universe is about balancing complementary opposites. The Universe balances the energy exchange between you and another because there's a part of you that's not understanding the true strength of your soul light. No-one can take this part of you away.

Coming back to 'doing the work', take Jesus as an example. One of the most holy men known. You would imagine he was high vibrational. You don't need to be a believer, but his story is inspiring. Jesus didn't hide from the world. He could've easily ostracized himself and just lived through life in divinity and do nothing about the corruption in the world. The people were clearly acting out of a lower frequency than him. Did that stop him? No. This was not his character. He knew his mission. He knew his purpose. He went out to the sick and the poor. He also liked to have a drink too. If you know and reflect upon his story, we are very similar. He too, was human. He was an example about how you can truly be divine having a physical experience.

Jesus loved and accepted even the most corrupt. I'm sure some people would have perceived them as low-vibe people. However, he was a beacon of hope that we all are worthy and deserving of a second chance no matter what we have done in our life. In the scribes it was the priests in the temples and the Pharisees who would preach that they were the Guru, yet their actions didn't reflect their words. There are probably a few people in the industry, whether it's religious or spiritual that you can think of that act like this too. They turned people away from 'the Church' and condemned some to death. They conspired to kill Jesus and got their wish because out of fear they weren't ready to face what wasn't congruent with what was truly emanating within their heart. They can be seen as a Master because of the hours of training they've put in, but does that mean that they truly represent what they master? Everyone is human. Every single person is an extension of the Divine. We are the paradox of both worlds. We are no less or more than another. We can only choose to become a leader of the Light and do our best in sticking towards what we know that assists the shift in human consciousness.

Earlier on in my awakening process, I demonstrated some of these qualities. I will own that. I needed to eat some humble pie. You might be this person, or you might know someone acting out like this. This is not judgement; it is giving insight and discernment to help navigate you to empower your soul. Don't follow my mistake and lose yourself so hard that you won't know who you are because you're living someone else's life which could be a complete fabrication. Don't become infatuated with someone else's values. Their gifts and purpose are completely different to yours. Your gifts will work perfectly for your soul Blueprint. If you're following the way of another, you may realise there's more blocks and it doesn't come as effortlessly. Live with respect and integrity for your soul. You don't need to prove your goodness or worth in this world. The fact you exist makes you already worthy. No matter what you do, say or learn, you are already making a difference without screaming from the mountains that you are a master. Always match your actions and intentions to make this world a better place.

Indicators of a Spiritual Ego in yourself or others:

* Making you mistrust your gift and intuition.
* Talks in jargon and unrealistic principles.
* Believes they are the highest vibrational being on this planet.
* Tells you some spiritual guidance that conflicts with your own intuition.
* Forgets to acknowledge their humanness.
* Disempowers your thoughts and actions.
* Their way is the only way.

IT'S NOT YOUR JOB

I wanted everyone to come along to the spiritual party! Early on anyway. I'm sure that my friends thought I was a nut job. I couldn't understand why anyone would *not* want to experience the bliss and peace that I was experiencing. I would take it personally when I tried to give them advice or show them what I learnt and they weren't interested or looked at me with judgement. I decided to change my actions. When I was in conversations I would briefly talk about my experiences and if they were curious, I would open up more. If not, then I wouldn't force my experiences onto them. At work, I began to keep things around my desk like crystals, affirmation and oracle cards which opened up more conversation. Whenever someone would ask me a question about it, only then would I show them my world gently. It was great because I began to meet more people who were open-minded, who I knew I could share my new life with.

Every single human is divinely destined to experience what their soul needs. Every person you meet has their own divine destiny. We aren't here to convince them that they have to go to a certain healer or do yoga. What works for *you* is what is pivotal to help *you* open up. Remember, there's nothing sexy about trying to push your beliefs onto someone else. If you keep doing what you're doing and the people you love are seeing such a transformation as you become your best Self, their curiosity will pique and open them up to this other world which could ultimately change their life. Allow people to live their path. If they're meant to journey with you, they will. If not, let them go. Sometimes it's just not your karma to resolve. Don't stick your finger in pies that aren't for you to stick them in!

Your change is for you alone. No-one else. The change you make influences everything around you. That's the change you create. Your job isn't to *fix* or *heal* anyone. If they're ready to come to the party they will. If not, they'll just choose not to respond to the R.S.V.P. and this is OKAY. If they choose to judge you, let them. You'd be surprised how many people who judged me earlier on in my spiritual journey and now have opened up to this world. Whether they decide to join me on this quest or not I still open my arms up to them, inviting them along because I know that our true purpose resides in being there for others. We are here to serve others, not just ourselves. Be a good human.

SOUL MASTERY INQUIRY

* Is there someone you're trying to put your new beliefs onto? Or you're pushing them away because you're trying to *fix* or *change* them?
* Who are the people you know who love to talk about what you're interested in? (This might not include your partner.)
* Finding at least one person who loves all that you love is a great release. If you don't know anyone *yet*, join a like-interest group and connect. Whether this is online or in-person.
* Release the need to change anyone. The only person we have control over is us.

GET GROUNDED

Isn't it funny how you can travel somewhere serene in nature and automatically feel the presence of the Divine in each and everything you perceive? There's no doubt that there's power and magic when we sit back and enjoy the wonder of creation that's all around us and we automatically come back into a sense of equilibrium within our being. I know that all I need to do to feel more connected to the Universe is to go to the ocean. I automatically start to feel that I am tapping back into the universal heartbeat of the Universe and earth.

The ability to be grounded can be the most underrated action that spirted people forget to do. As we invite more spirit in our life, we can become stuck in the stars and disconnected from the earth plane. It's easy to get lost up there. I always feel a sense of belonging in the stars. We have to be of this world, whilst bringing in the heavens. When you're feeling off-centre, it might not be that you haven't meditated enough, but rather the opposite.

If we are a soul having a human experience, we have to embrace both aspects—divine and physical.

Sometimes when you are feeling ungrounded it can be a sign that you are either future tripping or in the past. Earth is ruled by time. When we access Universal consciousness, we can be tapped into that effortless flow and feel that we are literally flying through the air. If you're 'floating' through life, you are too much in spirit and not grounded in this world. We want to bring heaven to earth. That's why we can access this part of our being. We are meant to. When you are purely focused in this present moment with conscious awareness, you are bringing that magical aspect of the Universe into this exact moment of time in your life. Integrated presence—soul and your physical body—is the united force and blessing that is being bestowed upon you but you need to be *all* here. It's easy to escape in the land of the mystics but when you bring that mystical presence to your everyday life in full immersion, it is as if you're grounded with magic and the natural rhythm of all that is in your physical body.

Signs that you may need to get grounded:

* Feeling airy fairy or dizzy.
* Not feeling connected to anyone or anything.
* Feeling off and slow.
* Feeling out of your body.
* Not present. You may find it hard to focus on the task at hand.
* Emotional instability.
* Feeling that your physical, mental and emotional state are moving too fast.

Ways to get grounded:

* Connect with nature.
* Breathe deeply.
* Be physical, exercise.
* Eat wholesome foods.
* Walk barefoot.
* Find a good hugger and hold them for thirty seconds or hug a tree.
* Drink water.
* Observe something that has a natural rhythm (the ocean crashing, the wind in the trees).
* Immerse your senses. What can you see, feel, hear, taste or smell? Do at least one sense per minute. Your awareness will come back to this present moment.

AUTHENTIC LIVING

If you strip away the ego as it loses itself in a crisis, what are you left with? The wisdom of perception. When you unplug from life you feel a deeper sense of awareness on the path of self-actualisation. Our level of awareness comes from where we are on a soul level and what we are meant to know and experience in this point of time in existence. It is why some people will show up with different levels of perception. How we see life depends on how we are willing to interpret the information we receive during our awakening process. With every layer we strip away and choose to see the blessing, only then can we truly understand the deep wisdom that our soul is expressing.

There will come a point where you can't live in a space that doesn't reflect who you are and what you value. When we aren't living authentically, it eats us up inside until we do something about it. We either act in a way that feels *right*, or we choose to continue to hide who we are, which leads to a downward spiral of shame, guilt, anger and sadness.

I understand that sometimes you might need to be in the spiritual closet to protect yourself in toxic environments or if something jeopardises your work, friends or family. If this is for you, give yourself a space where you can breathe and feel the authentic you!

The word 'authentic' comes from the Latin word meaning 'genuine'. The Greeks knew this word to mean 'original or primary'. Therefore, authenticity comes from your genuine, original Self. This stems from not the stories that you thought to believe about yourself, rather it is who you are at the core of your being—without societies influences on you.

How much is your life demonstrating your values? Determine what is important to you. Once you lift a layer of a subordinate illusion that's running you another layer will present itself. People are only pained by anything that's not in congruent with love and gratitude, the essence of who you are. Our physiology, mental state and emotions become a feedback system when things aren't congruent with your highest Self. It's the best communication system that things are not in alignment and this is great if we can recognise the signs that we are constantly given to move forward with our life. When the soul is in control, you can't keep living a lie or have that poker face on.

If you don't know what you value or who your authentic Self is then you could be living out someone else's values other than your own or comparing yourself to others instead of just being you. The world needs the most authentic version of you right now with no judgements of what you have or have not done. Your authentic Self is unapologetic, as every experience has been orchestrated from your divine plan for you to grow and flourish. Acting from the space of your most authentic Self feels like you can breathe because you are being you. This version may evolve over time. The most important part to focus on is to be your most authentic Self in this moment. This is your perfect you.

SOUL MASTERY LESSON

* Be unapologetic for following and believing in your truth.
* Your Truth will differ to others depending on their level of transformation and life experience.
* What feels right for us is what is for us.
* Authenticity will lead you into a deeper fulfilling life.
* Our physiology, emotions and mindset provide us feedback whether we are living congruently with our soul or not.
* Be you. Even if it feels illogical to others.

HONOUR YOURSELF

A spiritual awakening changes everything about you; what you thought you loved will change. Honour the process of what you're going through, what you're feeling, and honour others when they begin to see changes in you. It's often hard for others to understand what's happening to you, especially, if they knew you during your pre-awakened state. If they haven't experienced this sort of process themselves, they will not understand the change that is happening on all levels for you. They might've been the buddies you went out drinking with or caught up to gossip with. But now, this is not what fills your cup. Now, you have a sense of purpose and want substance in your life, not merely just to exist.

Every person who enters your life will serve a purpose. People come into your life for a reason, season or lifetime. When you're becoming your most authentic Self, the people who exist in your life, may not love and accept this version of you. This is okay. If they are unwilling to step up into unconditional love, then this will be the period where you'll begin to attract a like-minded soul family. It took me quite a few years of transition to bring in my kind of people. Let me tell you, it was hard letting go of friendships that fulfilled me for years. I had a shift in my being. I valued my time more than anything. I wanted to spend my moments in soulful experiences, rather than mediocre times. I got rid of my F.O.M.O. (Fear of Missing Out) and honoured how I was feeling.

I felt it was okay to miss out on events because I'd rather spend it listening to inspirational speakers or going to a workshop where I actually began to meet people who were just like me, going through a major transformation. Slowly, this just became a part of my life. A life that felt valuable. You have to be okay with the decisions you make that might not feel favourable to others, but you know within your heart and soul that it's the right choice for you.

There were times when I would go out and party. Then there were times where I would feel sick in my stomach not to do something and I honoured that. Each time I did this I found something would always happen. Whether it was an opportunity, meeting someone, having a deep healing, restoring my being, whatever it was, there would always be a reason and I'd always end up grateful that I didn't do something that didn't feel authentic to me. As time goes on, it becomes easier to recognise, accept and make decisions based on the integrity of your soul.

People may react negatively to your authentic Self and that is there choice to react this way. Their construct of you has totally changed and you've broken down their perceptions. You still have an element of ensuring that you act respectful in the way you authentically respond to your calling when in the presence of others. With dignity, explain the truth in what you're feeling and that this isn't about them. Your path is your own. Only you can answer the calling, not them. If you act out of accordance to please someone else's desires, then you risk emotional, mental and physical imbalances, a healing crisis or resentment. There is a reason for you needing some *you* time. It might be an important time for your integration process. Trust this. Have faith and know you are divinely loved, supported and guided to live out the life you're meant to live.

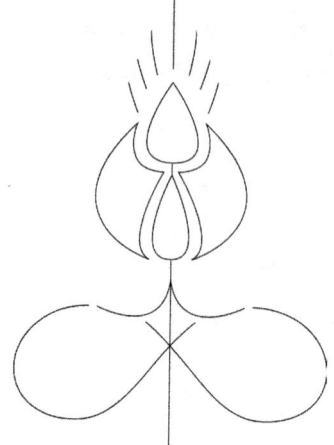

BE UNAPOLOGETIC FOR BEING AUTHENTIC, HONOUR YOURSELF IN EACH AND EVERY MOMENT.

GROWING THROUGH CHALLENGES

No challenge; no soul growth.

I got a new job in my thirties as a Student Wellbeing Leader in a Primary School. I thought that my role would be straightforward. As the new kid on the block, and like any workplace, people in positions of power can either help you thrive or test you. Every day there seemed to be a new challenge. I had received jobs to do that weren't in my job description. As someone very aware of my energy, I know that when we are pulled in too many directions, we *can* become very unproductive. Clarity brings conviction; uncertainty brings doubt. I even received jobs from other specialist areas that weren't my role, but they tried to handball it down as if it had some form of connection to what I was doing. Anyone can spin that there's a relationship between wellbeing and a role that needs to be done.

Let me tell you, it left me pissed off. I was happy to be at work, but when I feel that people are out of integrity it rubs me the wrong way. I'm aligned with truth—authenticity, integrity and Light—when something is not in this space, then this is when I feel I need to act. However, being new, I didn't know who I could trust or gain insights from on how to tackle things. I had to be careful with what I said and to whom because I know how words can be used against us. I was slowly gaining traction on who I couldn't trust. It didn't mean that I would treat them poorly, it just meant that I would continue being myself. Yet, I was wary of my words and actions around them. The to-dos list continued to pile on of jobs I had no idea how to even complete. I had a lack of passion and experience in what they were asking me to do. I truly believe that good leadership is understanding your staff. Understanding someone's gifts and talents and giving people jobs that they are passionate about. I will do anything for anyone and if I'm unsure I'm much more hesitant to go in. If I'm in a role to create change and my talents are not being utilised to their full potential, then that's when I will feel off-centre.

So, I thought, *I can either sink or rise.* I needed a plan of attack. I had pent up anger that was making me more unproductive. I asked Spirit for assistance. To help me to either shift my perspective or send the help that I need to get things done. My theme for the year was to have courage. To do what brought me out of my comfort zone. I used this opportunity to learn. Every job I received all seemed to be what my weaknesses were. *What if I turned these weaknesses into strengths? What if I was able to overcome this challenge?*

On our path we have to show up. We might not like the assignments we receive, but the feeling of achieving them might bring about the best experience we could ever imagine. Whether they turn out or not it's not the outcome that matters, but what we can gain from the journey. You have to work hard to get the diamond. Your soul is brave. Your soul is courageous. Every assignment sent your way is one that you'll always be able to pass. That experience will bring out more of you. You may need to release the idea of what a 'pass' mark is for you. Expectations are the cause of our downfall and the cause of our negative self-talk. Be easy on yourself. Have courage and know that when you've put in the effort and nothing changes it just means that you are now in a space of changing to something even greater.

Challenges support us to grow and gears us to where we need to be next for our life path. How many times have you had something happen to you and in hindsight it was the best thing because it brought you to where you are today? We are not victims of our life. Don't buy into that or that will become your story which will further disempower you. We are just becoming aware of where we may be disempowered. The Universe is about balance and harmony. We balance out the aspect of ourselves that needs to reach the point of presence, centeredness and attention. Here we can produce powerful alchemy to transform our life. I successfully survived that year of manic and I was so grateful for all the new skills I learned along that way. That experience also helped me to move into my new job. I also knew that if I could transcend the uncomfortable feeling on doing jobs that I found challenging then when it came to do these sorts of tasks in a job that was aligned to my dreams, I would have enough courage to work through my feelings. Try and shift your perception to help you sift through one present issue, now. Challenges offer you an opportunity to grow. You can grow through what you go through. There is nothing you can't handle and in time you may just see that this was the best thing that ever happened *for* you.

SOUL MASTERY INQUIRY

* How can I learn from this experience?
* What blessings does this challenge bring me?
* What would be the highest perspective I could have from this

perceived challenged?
* What steps would I need to do to overcome it?
* What gift would I receive from having the courage to conquer this challenge?

IT'S OKAY NOT TO BE OKAY

When heartache comes, we often feel guilty for not surviving and struggling. We have been conditioned to think that it's weak to accept help and we can feel helpless when we encounter negative emotions and experiences. Don't judge yourself if you're going through the hard times and are *not* coping. You're allowed to feel sorry for yourself. However, there is a fine line between staying stuck in the story and allowing you to feel what's necessary for your transformation. Acceptance is what helps bring you back into presence and tapping into the flow of where you need to be next. Resisting your pain will only bring it further into your awareness and make you feel guilty.

COPING WITH DRASTIC CHANGES

When everything happens all at once, we tend to feel like we've been knocked off our centre. Some changes will provoke an aspect of your being that feels it can no longer support that which doesn't fulfil your soul. The pain can feel more intense when we have circumstances that come from out of the blue. It's like a nuclear bomb that's destroyed a part or our whole world. When we feel like we are not in control of our life, it can be really scary and uncomfortable. Fear into the unknown is normal. If we could see the divine presence that resides on the other side of fear, we would feel comfort in knowing that everything is working in our favour. When events occur that shake us up, we have to be committed to staying strong to our authentic Self. We can easily be led astray to the drama storm that comes from uncertainty. Be aware of any feelings that come up for you during a time of change.

Awareness comes in the absence of judgement. It just is. If there's an emotional charge towards your thoughts, it is an important thing to note. An awakening to consciousness brings about the awareness of your unconscious Self. These thoughts and emotional triggers act as an opportunity to heal. The opportunity to transcend the emotional charge from a thought—a mental construction of the mind—is a blessed process. Don't fight whatever comes to you. Thank what presents itself to you as a gift to heal. Any resistance only produces more resistance to your being which will result in the struggle to feel a sense of control of the Self. Chaos. The fact it has come into your consciousness is a good thing. Over time, you'll see how the same circumstance has a less emotional charge, take the time to acknowledge the hard work you've done in working to be your best Self—your most self-actualised Self. Getting back to centre becomes quicker. The transcendence of the mind's perception of uncontrolled change comes with the understanding and opportunity to see the blessing that has opened up an opportunity for more of the divine presence to shine through.

> **When the change becomes unbearable and you need help shifting, ask for a divine presence to intervene.**

My workplace was becoming unbearable. I was trying to hide from some people in leadership because they were on a rampage that if you tried to interact with them they would slam you. I was ghosting deliberately. Just trying to do my thing but so many people were getting called into the office to be told off for all the things they weren't doing well. Midway through the year, three teachers ended up resigning in the same week which rang alarm bells considering it was a small school. That just highlighted how toxic the environment was. A few weeks before, I had asked the Holy Spirit to come through to help heal the workplace. I always call on the Holy Spirit when I really need something cleared up. It's non-discriminatory and anyone can call upon it. I see it as a pure Spirit that comes from the Divine and it tends to act quickly. I know that whenever I hand things over to the Holy Spirit that things get working. This is not to say that it was the cause of the resignations, I was really sad to see these wonderful people leave the workplace. However, it acted as a catalyst for those who were causing grief to some of the staff members, an opportunity to heal and reflect. It became their awakening. The truth and integrity of the spirit will always come through.

IN DIFFICULT TIMES, ASK THE HOLY SPIRIT OR A HIGHER PRESENCE TO WORK ITS MAGIC.

THE DRAMA STORM

Some storms you aren't meant to be a part of. If others are experiencing some form of change it might not mean that you're meant to be a part of the change. It may be just a part of their journey.

The important aspect is to give yourself space. Get into stillness to access your centre. This part of you helps you to make the best choices for your soul. You'll know when it's time to move on when every part of your being feels like it's somewhere else. If there's a thought that you'll be leaving with unfinished business, explore that. Your time may not be now.

While in the chaos at my work, close friends would ask, 'How was your day?' I'd reply with, 'I ghosted all day, successfully!' A drama storm can be like a game of tag. If you choose to play and get in it there's a likely chance you'll get *tagged*. People want to pass it on. I'd ask Spirit to make me invisible throughout the day, like in Harry Potter and his invisibility cloak moving through Hogwarts. I'd laugh when someone would try to find me, they couldn't see me even if I was only a few metres away. *Thank you, Spirit!* I wasn't doing this out of fear, but conservation of keeping my energy flowing positively.

I focused on what needed to be done, instead of getting stuck in the drama storm which isn't helpful or beneficial for my path. The drama storm drags us down to our lower Self. Love yourself enough to know that we have to honour everyone's journey. We don't need to create unnecessary karma or emotional distress if it's not warranted. We don't need to attach ourselves to a lower vibration. We can hold space for others to rise during this time. Stay detached, empathetic and have an open and compassionate heart. In this state, we give the opportunity for others to transition smoothly.

Others being in your presence will automatically cause a stir in their auric field to adjust to their Higher Self. The ego will do anything to resist Spirit. When the ego is in control, lower emotions and traits are amplified in an individual. Still, be the light. Stay in your pillar. Let nothing—no thing—move your internal reference to your true Self.

Be so Light, be so bright that people who enter your presence automatically shift into the vibration of being authentic to their Higher Self. This may bring about their biggest ego, it might not even be directly at you, but don't let it destroy your peace.

THE DIVINE PRESENCE

Making time for your soul is the greatest gift you can give to yourself and others. It's the moments of stillness that brings you back into the now. The now is one of the most potent places to create from. Whilst it's important to reflect on the learnings of the past and set the intentions for what we want for the future, if we are spending too much time in moments that aren't existing in the now, we can miss opportunities of beauty, grace, magic, joy and flow.

It is in the now that nothing else exists other than what conscious choice you make. Your now is determined by all the conscious choices you *have* made. If you don't like where you're heading, manifest your energy back to stability, to a creation point, and shift the momentum where you want it to go. The most potent creative energy happens in that moment of stillness—that gap, the void—the presence in between. Like the flow of the breath, when we inhale and exhale there is a point of stillness that helps to shift and stabilize your energy. The power of the breath allows you to slow down to make better decisions, as you are run by the power of your unlimited Spirit rather than the power of your limited mind. Deep breathing allows the voice of your Spirit to become louder, so you can create more of a spirited life, rather than being run by the conditions of the world.

When you go on a holiday, you take more moments to soak up a new environment. Presence allows us to feel that we are taking a holiday every day, in every moment. It's like being in *The Matrix* in slow mode with an increased awareness of how each and every *thing* around you is truly magical. The magic of slowing down our breathing allows us to slow down time to get us faster into our heart space.

Our heart is one of the most potent organs in our body symbolically, energetically and physically. The heart space is where the presence of the Divine resides. From here, every decision, thought and action we take from the heart comes from the right place. In the heart space, only love exists. Therefore, everything that you consciously choose to do and make is going to be for the highest good of all. Your awareness expands. Presence assimilates into your field and being. Shifting your perspective to that of loving and accepting each moment brings about a powerful focus in the now.

In a society that glorifies multi-tasking, it does more damage that good as it activates our instinctual brain instead of using the part of our brain that allows for self-regulation, insight and higher cognitive functioning. How do you become more present? In every thought and action that you do, choose to do that one thing with all your attention. If someone is talking, listen without interrupting and ask them to tell you more. If you've got a few projects you need to complete, focus on the one that's most important and needs to be done now. If you're going for a walk, don't bring your phone, just be present with what surrounds you. You'll find that you'll get better quality work, achievements and your overall outlook on life.

What happens to your energy is that it goes everywhere if your thoughts are everywhere. Our thoughts are there to help direct intentional energy where it needs to go. When we have too much on it creates overwhelm. Overwhelm is a sign that our energy is everywhere, and we have to bring presence back to bring about stability. If you've been running scattered for a while, it will take commitment, discipline and focus to redirect back the course of your flow.

My grandmother would say, especially when it came to cooking, 'If you're going to do something do it properly or not at all.' I think she had a clue about being present. Whatever we enter, whether it's a job, project, exercise, eating food, being with friends, talking, thoughts or actions, enter it with the greatest presence you can bring. Try it yourself. Social media and technology are one of our biggest distractors when it comes to presence. Put away your phone when you're catching up with friends or wanting to complete a project. It's easy to get lost in the cyber world. As we choose to become more present, the 'real' world becomes more glorified than the 'cyber reality' which so many people get lost in.

Create a mission for the week to focus on one thing at a time with your full attention. In your present state, you may even discover some patterns, habits, actions or thoughts that you were unaware of that may need to shift. You may even notice that you're more relaxed, inspired and have more energy throughout the day.

Now, for the creatives. Focusing on just one thing is especially important for those who feel that they get creative ideas all the time. My mentors would tell me, 'just focus on one thing'. I found this harder to do as I thought I didn't want my creative ideas to leave and someone else to take them. As creativity comes from the stream of universal consciousness. One of my mentors said that if I didn't focus on just one thing, then I'd never complete anything that I was here to do. It's like running a sprinting race and having to run another lap again because there's no finish line. From seeing the result of no results, only unfinished work, it was big for me to just focus on one thing.

How can you decide what to work on? I'd work on what expanded my heart which then felt effortless. I had three book ideas and wasn't sure where to start. So, I began to write what made me feel most energized. As I worked, I had to create time in my schedule for creative time. I set the intention in that space that I would focus on writing the book that needed to be done. Every week at the same time ideas for this book would just flow. It made me realise how important it is just to be present. In terms of creativity, I realised how important it is for it to become a non-negotiable for time to be present with your soul. In the past, I would give up the opportunity of my time to be taken over by others, not anymore. You have to be committed to the cause. I have seen so many of my friends become successful because they were committed to being present in whatever needed to be done. When we would catch up, they would be 'all there' because they had taken time to finish what they needed to get done. There are moments where I might get insights for my other creative projects. I don't dismiss them. I write them down and I know at the right time they will be worked on next. Presence is intentional focus. In presence, without a doubt, you know the Divine is in each and every moment.

SOUL MASTERY LESSON

* Focus on one activity for a period of time.
* Give all your attention to just *one* thing.

* When conversing with someone, listen and consciously choose to be 'all there' and feel a difference in the conversation.
* Focus on what energizes you.
* For creatives, choose one project to work on and create a time in your schedule to work on that one thing.

INCREASE IN SENSITIVITY

As you continue on your healing journey, you will release layer upon layer. You, in essence, become lighter. Your 'light' body is lighter because more of your soul essence is able to filter through. You become more attuned with Universal flow. However, all of this comes with a warning that you'll never be the same again. You'll feel when what's around you feels dense and this may make you want to retreat. Your sensitivity is your gift to help you understand and navigate the next steps in your path.

Months before I went to John of God, I started noticing that I couldn't go outside in public without feeling as if a vacuum was sucking all my energy up. As soon as I would retreat home everything would be okay. It was as if my sanctuary was a healing pod of protection and rejuvenation. I didn't understand what was happening. I was unaware that this was in preparation for my deepest healing to occur. We are constantly being better versions of ourselves. If people had known, they'd probably have thought I was going through a depression. I wouldn't go out or see anyone. I would sit at home and either cry or just prefer my own company. People of my past knew me as an extrovert who would go out and party in an instant. So, this was out of character for me. My favourite place to be in my house was in a fetal position in bed praying that I would feel better.

I wanted all the painful memories that kept coming up to stop but I knew that if I was truly dedicated to this path and wanted to attract what my heart desired, a part of me needed to die. To die to allow the trinity of the mind, body and soul to merge by working together in harmony. Therefore, the aspect of me that didn't honour all of these parts came up to be illuminated. As we learned earlier on it's through solitude that you can hear or feel what your soul desires. However, it is when you become attuned to the life force that flows through you that you will find what either allows you to fly or makes you sink. For me, I had to give up saying yes to everyone and begin by saying yes to me. This meant that I needed to miss some social engagements and I was okay with that.

This sensitivity that you may feel or are feeling needs to be honoured. If you're feeling depleted, it's because you are! When did you not honour yourself? Was it hanging around a toxic friend because you felt obliged? Going to a social event because it was the right thing to do? Your sensitivity is a sign of preventative *HEAL*th measures to keep all of you in balance and harmony. I wanted to highlight the *heal* part in *heal*th to remind you that your healing is up to you. As you develop this sensitivity, you are becoming deeply self-aware of yourself and what you need. We are developing the instincts of our ancient ancestors who understood the balance of life and had a 'light' lifestyle.

It's all about making lighter choices and discern what that means for you. Healthy—less processed food, more exercise, meditation, routine, healthy relationships, positive mindsets, purposeful career—a balanced lifestyle all play a part and assist with keeping your light body maintained. We all know that this is good for you but what is knowledge if you don't apply its wisdom? It can be hard to do all of it at once. When you make it a part of who you are, because it is, then life becomes more effortless. You will feel clear, strong and balanced. Your intuition will become stronger and you will notice that the synchronicities in your life become more frequent because there is no separation from you and Source. You're closer to Source because you are lighter. What do we always get told to do? Focus on the Light.

If you're finding it hard to understand what is happening to you, then know that all you need to do is give yourself permission to feel exactly what you're feeling. If you want to go home and cry, do so. If you feel that you don't want to go out, that's okay too. Trust how you're feeling and know that it's okay. Don't believe that this is going to be your life forever because we know this is not your truth. Remember that, 'this too shall pass.' Your mind and body need time to catch up with your soul and when you feel like you're absorbing the world, you are in need of a period of time in solitude to rest, rejuvenate and then get into full momentum again in the world.

Increases in your sensitivity include:

* Physical. Changes in your foods, bodily reactions to certain experiences, people or places.
* Emotional. Much more vulnerable, open, can cry easily, sense other people's feelings.
* Intuition. Feeling and knowing clearer guidance.

ENERGETIC BOUNDARIES

First, respect your energetic boundaries. As every person and place that we've encountered creates an energetic attachment. These are forms of memories that you can tap into any time. They can be sources of inspiration or despair. Unconsciously, we can have energetic holes in our auric layer that can seep through and feed people or space that we may have had an energetic connection to. The hardest part is that we may be unaware that it's occurring. It can be masked as fatigue, anxiety, tightness in the tummy, or feeling drained. This is why it's important to be constantly tuning in and connecting in with our intuition. It is through stillness that we can begin to receive guidance on what we might be giving our power away to and then act on how to tighten up where we want our flow to go.

> **Are you giving your power away, or leaking energy right now?**

Whatever we place our attention on is where our flow of energy is going. You must begin to see that you are not the source or have an unlimited supply to give. In order to give you must regenerate. Your boundaries act as what you allow or don't allow in your auric field so it's important to be clear. What do you allow in your space? What are you unconsciously allowing to come through? How can you allow more space for what you want? Imagine your energetic boundaries as a sacred container. There is only so much that you can fit in it until it overflows. If we are stuffing it with too much stuff, then we risk the container cracking. This can include when we are taking too much on or continuously thinking about others who lower our vibe. I want you to imagine that we can only hold onto a certain amount of *stuff* every time you continue to commit to something in your mind, heart and through what you choose to do each day. Therefore, we have to be mindful about what we consciously allow in and how we choose to spend our thoughts and actions. Even when we are feeling empowered and doing things we love, if we are saying yes to too many things, our energy becomes scattered. Remember, your energy is a sacred supply and we have to become clearer in what we commit to.

If you're stuck thinking about another person and how much wrong they did to you, then guess what, your energy is leaking there. That's what you're filling your sacred container with. Wouldn't you rather be spending it on something that uplifts you? When our consciousness drifts to a time, place or person who lowers our vibe, we dial right into that energy. You literally are creating a cord of suction to start taking away your energy. When we empower all parts and dimensions of who we are and consciously choose where we direct our energy and what we allow it to be spent on, we become less likely to be affected by those who do like to 'vamp' right into our energy field because that acts as your barrier. You set the intentions of what you allow or don't allow. All parts that make up your energy has a ripple effect. Your mindset affects your emotions and physiology. Your physiology can affect your mind and emotions. This creates a ripple effect for your overall energy and can influence your ability to hear your intuition's guidance. If you've created a strong mindset, those people who you feel overpower you have no control over you. Therefore, they don't have any influence on you anymore. You've created this intentional thought field that they no longer can take or lower your energy.

> **Your intentional boundaries act as your energetic gatekeeper.**

The way to protect ourselves from energy vamping is to be clear about our boundaries and become stronger where we might allow a leak of energy to occur. Vamping might not always appear in a person. It can include being immersed in too many projects or completely dwelling on something whether it is past, present or future. It can even come from being too accessible to someone you dearly care about and have trouble saying no to. We are becoming intentionally conscious with where we direct our energy.

> **We are the gatekeeper of our energetic system. Protect yourself from energetic vamping.**

When I was ending my time at work, I started noticing that my energy was depleted as soon as I walked in each morning. I am always aware of how I show up each day. I would go to school in an inspired state, then as soon as I stepped foot in the workplace it was as if my soul light was being drained heavily.

Months later, I felt a divine intervention. I started to receive clarity on what was happening. My Light body couldn't handle the density of the space. However, there was something greater that I didn't know on another level. I had focused my healing on resolving contracts to be healed and restored on all layers. It wasn't until I had a dream that everything became clear. I kept dreaming about work and even though I had already set the intention to clear and resolve any karmic debts, I was still energetically linked to them. In each dream, I was slowly detaching from their energy and Spirit was showing me not to look back. I was happily saying goodbye and I saw others who should leave the workplace and were holding off another year as it was a part of their soul contract. The part of the dream that startled me was that I dreamt of my now ex-colleagues. Here, they all looked terrible, almost zombie like. They looked starved and soulless. In my dream, I was waiting for a plane to go to the Sunshine Coast in Queensland. I could see that there was a light coming from my back as I felt in an inspired state. As I started to leave, someone grabbed my arm and said, 'I love your energy.' In that moment, I felt that I was actually feeding them because they weren't able to find the light and align themselves to a different pure Source where true energy flows from.

Suddenly, I felt all of my soul power come through and then I firmly telepathically stated, *I will no longer give you permission to feed off me.* I knew if they looked to me as a Source, then they're misguided on finding their true Light. I was holding so much energetically for them for so long—for peace and harmony—they now had to be confronted with holding the fort down for themselves. Then, I saw chaos occur, people fighting, running around everywhere, it was like a crazy circus. I felt an incredible power as I rose and what I can only describe as uniting my full soul power. I stood up with so much authority and a thunderous sound came out. With conviction I said, 'This needs to stop.' As soon as I spoke, everyone looked at me in silence. I felt a sense of healing rush through everyone like my words were a sound bath and everyone in its frequency was able to receive that transmission. I saw everyone in agreeance. Then a glimmer of hope and inspiration came when a male colleague stood up and started to speak. When he spoke, he encouraged everyone to be positive and did an amazing inspirational speech. Everyone began to change. I knew my work was done.

I woke up feeling more energized than before. It was as if all my soul fragments had come back to me that I had lost or given to others. It was only the day before that I had thought Spirit Filled Thoughts, SFT, *I no longer give permission for my energy body to be used as a source of light, or to hold anyone, in places that are no longer for my highest good or in my soul contract from this and any other lifetime or in any other dimension.*

From this experience I understood that setting energetic boundaries is so important in order for us to move forward. If we don't it may slow us moving forward. Our body is the only vehicle we have that navigates us through our world. Reclaiming the power of your soul is an essential part in assuring that you're able to move forward with conviction and fulfil your soul purpose.

SOUL MASTERY INQUIRY

* What are you consciously or unconsciously giving permission for your energy to go to?
* Have you given your power away to anyone?
* Are you carrying someone emotionally or energetically because you don't want them to suffer but you're suffering instead?
* Are your thoughts and actions coming from you, or has it been influenced by another because your boundaries have been compromised?

* Remember, what are you holding in your sacred container? Are you overcommitting or have you discovered the right balance?
* Set your intentions for what you allow and don't allow in your time, space and energy.

DECLARE WHAT YOU WILL OR WILL NOT ALLOW IN YOUR ENERGETIC FIELD.

SET FIRM BOUNDARIES.

ENERGETIC SELF-CARE

I am a yes person (although, I've gotten better at saying no!). I hate letting people down. But by doing so, I run the risk of letting me down by becoming so depleted and drained that I need to take time to feel normal again! This is why it is so important to be clear about our boundaries. But we have to know how much to give to ourselves is in the order to keep our vitality and wellbeing health. Sometimes we might give a lot of ourselves without even realising. I know too that I'm guilty of overcommitting. This can even be to things which might bring me joy when my soul is telling me to rest and I'm not listening.

Yet we can forget that there's only one you and only one of you to carry out your sacred mission. Your awakening establishes for you what isn't in alignment with you anymore and how to ensure that you nurture this sacred vessel to carry out your mission. We might've been taught to give so much to the world, that we completely forget what matters to us. We can lose our identity and our sense of self when we live of the world, rather than taking the time to live the way of spirit. Your self-care practice ensures that you are giving yourself time to reset. Are you becoming extremely emotional or sensitive? Or have this nagging feeling to do something and not know how to act or what to do? Your body feels completely exhausted, but you continue to grab that cup of coffee to give you that extra energy hit when what you really need is a rest? We have all been here I know that I have myself and there comes to a point where we have had enough. This can sometimes manifest in a way which you might start to get some physical signs that things are beginning to get out of control.

But we can't wait for disaster to strike to start thinking, "Hey I better act and make some changes." You have to pull in the reigns a lot earlier than this. That's why our boundaries become so important. Some conditions can become irreversible and you can't wait until disaster hits to make a change.

> Make that change now.
> If you tuned into your body right now, how does it feel?
> Are you tired? Do you have any tension in your body?
> Or do you feel agitated or full of energy? How's the pace of your breath?

Now let's connect into your mind. What are you thinking of? What are some of your thoughts? Are you thinking about all the things you need to do? Are you thinking nothing? Whatever it is this is okay.

That moment of pausing is activating our parasympathetic nervous system to calm down and to restore back to balance. It allows the brain to slow down so that it can come from a place of higher judgement, rather than irrationality. That pause and stillness, that moment between breaths is like the space of the soul and it's no wonder that we can get some creative insights, ideas and guidance in the oddest of times like the shower, when you're walking, driving. Your mind has been given time to access your intuition. So, we have to ensure that we take care of your beautiful self because there is only one you.

We also have a certain amount of energy that we have each day. Imagine your energy like a bank account. If we are constantly having people take from us or we are giving too much, you'll end up being in debt and the same can be said about our energy.

The more we allow ourselves to receive, we are allowing a deposit to be made in our account. Constant deposits and savings allow your money (which is your energy) into surplus. There is an abundant amount which allows you to not feel drained or any other yucky feelings.

The body will tell you when it's had enough through physical symptoms such as anxiety or fatigue. You can't keep pushing something that has nothing more to give. So, we have to ensure that you take care of your beautiful self. Especially if you're a giver, self-care allows you to receive and it's time that you gave yourself permission to receive, including a compliment (I know some of you may cringe at that thought and you're the ones I'm talking to that need to look after yourself!). You are not selfish for looking after you. It is a necessity for surviving and thriving.

SOUL MASTERY INQUIRY

* Remember that you have a limited supply of energy. Take care of it. There are different types of self-care. Nurture your physical, emotional, and spiritual sides.
* What recharges you?
* How to keep up your self-care practice.
* Establish your boundaries.
* Schedule some time for you. What will you do for yourself daily? Weekly? Monthly?

- Commit to this!
- Grab a journal and finish these sentences:

    If I dedicated time to myself, I would feel . . .

    My relationships will . . .

    My life would become . . .

    My energy would be . . .

ENERGETIC DETOX

When we care about someone or many people, we of course, are the Light to show them the way. We energetically support them to assist them on their journey. They can rely on our energetic source rather than learning about their own. We might do this unintentionally. It's the reason why we sometimes need an energetic detox. If we are in dire need to purge it will occur.

I had to use that powerful declaration for my soul in claiming back my energy as I was entering a new cycle in my life. I know how I AM in an inspired state. I need to bring that wherever I go. I had lost my spark as my being was being battered in this place that greatly needed the light. I know that I did my best, but I was burnt out from the people who were unwilling to change, and I felt that I wasn't free. My dream space was where I could recharge my batteries. That's why a good sleep routine is so important. Your soul has space to regenerate as your mind, body and emotions catch up. I felt rejuvenated, even though my mind and emotions were feeling broken.

It's so important to work on your pillar of light during this period of time if you're going through any of this. If you're in a job or relationships that you feel are sucking the life out of you, stay true to your alignment. There's a chance that it's a sign that you'll need to move on or create change. Whether you know it's your time or not; alignment is always the key. Keep aligned to Source and know that the Universe will always have your back. The right job or person or experience will come to you in the right time. Surrendering to a greater power is what this process is all about, so you can tap into more Universal flow, frequently.

Whether we are on social media, meeting friends or others, watching television, or going to particular places, we are soaking up energy. The best way to reset is to give yourself space to rejuvenate. If you're going through a deep processing stage, your high sensitivity may mean you are feeling everything around you more than usual. It might even be that if you watch something that brings you down, this will affect your energy. If you open up social media and someone writes a sad post it can affect your mood and energy levels. The ancients always practiced some form of detox. Sometimes the process can be a little painful, but you will always feel the rewards later. The benefits of an energetic detox are that it also allows you to detach from anything that might have become an addiction, which could have been slowing down the process of your Soul Blueprint. This is your integration period and if this is happening, give yourself space to be. Your vitality can be in a direct relationship with how you treat yourself.

To look after your energy body and to give yourself an energetic detox:

State your intentions with conviction.

Give yourself some solitude time.

Rest, rest, rest.

Hydrate.

> Get physical.
> Be committed to staying in flow and in an inspired state.
> Listen to an inspired speaker.
> Connect with people who uplift you.
> Clear up your environment.

SOUL MASTERY AFFIRMATION

"I am in full alignment to my divine purpose and know that anything that is no longer serving me or supporting me for my purpose that a diving intervention is at play that will lead me to the right experience, which will help my soul to flourish and thrive. And so, it is."

Repeat x 3.

"I am in full alignment to my divine purpose and know that anything that is no longer serving me or supporting me for my purpose that a diving intervention is at play that will lead me to the right experience, which will help my soul to flourish and thrive. And so, it is."

"I am in full alignment to my divine purpose and know that anything that is no longer serving me or supporting me for my purpose that a diving intervention is at play that will lead me to the right experience, which will help my soul to flourish and thrive. And so, it is."

"I am in full alignment to my divine purpose and know that anything that is no longer serving me or supporting me for my purpose that a diving intervention is at play that will lead me to the right experience, which will help my soul to flourish and thrive. And so, it is."

FORGIVENESS

The past can feel like dark clouds hovering above you wherever you go. They in form can be any person or circumstance that you are *unwilling* to forgive and release. They weigh upon you. Bitterness blackens the heart and it can feel like a disease. It can take months, perhaps years for a breakthrough to come through. It can be hard to let go of that hurt and the anger or sadness and it can stir you up inside. To truly forgive someone means that when you think about this person, there is a sense of understanding about their purpose in your life, and peace is within your heart. If you're unable to forgive, you are stuck in chaos. It might even be the reason, without you realising, why a relationship isn't working, or you feel there's no forward momentum in your life.

To forgive, you're not saying that whatever was done to you or the circumstances that occurred was okay, but instead you are finding peace within your whole being because it's what you deserve. You deserve peace of mind and heart. Without forgiveness you're holding onto the past that no longer exists in this present moment. Wouldn't you rather let it go? Forgiveness is one of the greatest gifts we can give to ourselves and others. Life is sweet. An unforgiving heart leaves you with a bitter taste on life.

Like you, I'm sure you've had people who've betrayed and done things against you. It not only makes you feel disappointed, but it can really affect the way in which you operate in the world. It can take you out of the heart space immediately. It's the people closest to you that tend to hurt you the most or someone you've trusted. It's understandable that in your hurt state you're going to find it much more difficult to see the blessing that they have given you.

There's a passage in the Bible, the gospel according to Matthew, where Peter asks Jesus how many times he should forgive his brothers or sisters who've sinned against him. "Should it be seven?" Jesus answers, "Not seven times, seventy-seven times." What does this tell us about forgiveness? That it takes time. You can say to someone 'I forgive you' because you want peace, but it might take time over and over again, repeating this to yourself, until you can finally be at peace with whatever has occurred. Don't be hard on yourself if you haven't been able to do it instantly. Just be willing.

As much as it's important to forgive others, you have to be able to give that grace to yourself. You deserve that peace too. We aren't perfect. We have all done or said something that has hurt someone. Sometimes your actions will be used as a change agent for others and that's been used in the divine plan as well. Every person who comes into our life and has the potential to hurt us, actually has an immense love for us as a soul. All things are destined to create you into the best human being possible. Treat each hurt with the fragility that it is. Hold it gently. Go there when you feel strong enough emotionally and mentally to tackle it.

On occasions, we can displace what others have done to us onto others because we've allowed the bitterness to carry on. If you want to break that cycle you have to do the work. When you learn to forgive, you are declaring as a powerful soul that you can transcend this learning, so it doesn't keep happening to you.

I had a dream that I had gathered a whole soul family together. Present, were two sisters, who I know in reality have been fighting for so long that their lives were being affected because they held onto so much anger, resentment, bitterness and jealousy. It divided the family because which side do you choose to take? Most people are influenced by the side with the most power. As they all gathered together, I started talking about how this needed to stop. I could feel that if they didn't work it all out in this lifetime, they would have to come again to work out the lesson. Some of the family that was present began to walk out of the room and I said that those who were choosing to walk away from the truth and the path of forgiveness were the ones who really needed to listen. I felt that they were working on some other lessons. Then it was only left to the two sisters and their immediate family. All of a sudden, I began to recite the prayer of St Francis of Assisi. I reiterated this line: "Where there is hatred, let me sow love." After that was declared, we all went into the kitchen and it was as if everything was resolved. There are times when things can just be enough and we have to come together to declare, let us seek love now so we can all move on. I always think, I'd rather work things out now, than have to come back another lifetime with someone you dislike. Do your best to work on your feelings towards someone. There are circumstances that will occur, where you are reminded of this person. This is an opportunity and gateway for your healing to occur. It's not the Universe punishing you, it's a sign that this is what needs peace.

Are you bringing others with you because of your resentment? We are all part of the divine plan. Whatever has happened between you and another was meant to happen. Don't drag others into your battle. You can feel supported without someone hating another person. Be the bigger person. It's an uncomfortable position for anyone to take a side with someone they may be close to as well. People have to be given permission to live their own journey and to base their opinions on someone else. A person might treat you like crap but another like gold. Again, we don't know what's going on in another's life. We can only make assumptions. If you're that person stuck in the middle, stay centred and detach from any other influence. Stay true to your own sense of perception of reality. Offer a space for healing to occur.

Staying bitter keeps you stuck. Like a hamster running on a wheel. You repeat the same story and that's the only story that keeps being played in your mind. If you want a new story, you have to create it and it starts with peace. The ending of your life movie does not need to end with you only focused solely on the problem, because every good story has a turning point, a solution to the problem. You are the solution to your peace. If you keep giving to the same person who has caused you pain, you are only giving yourself more grief. If it's someone you can't avoid, the only thing you can work on is your mindset.

Why do I give a whole part to forgiveness? Because if you truly utilise the power of forgiveness, you'll begin to see a transformation in the way that you live. You become lighter and receive more blessings that the Universe has to offer. Hand it over to the Universe if you still feel it lingering on. It's okay if you thought you let it go and it comes back again. The feelings of hate, anger, resentment or hurt might not disappear straight away, but having an intention to be released from you is the biggest step you can make on your path. It just means that you're ready to take it to a new level. Dig deeper and release it for good. Remember, it will take more than only seven times to forgive just one thing! Stop causing your own suffering and let peace and love enter.

> ### SOUL MASTERY LESSON
>
> Hand it over to Spirit. Ask for a divine intervention to occur for you to shift your perceptions on this event and for all your karma to be complete. Ask for a higher perspective to come through for you. The Universe will always deliver. Thank the Universe for delivering an enlightened perspective. You don't need to suffer anymore.

If you're finding it hard to forgive, say the *Prayer of St Francis of Assisi* to begin the flow of peace to enter your life.

"Lord, make me an instrument of your peace.
Where there is hatred, let me sow love;
Where there is injury, pardon;
Where there is discord, union;
Where there is doubt, faith;
Where there is despair, hope;
Where there is darkness, light;
Where there is sadness, joy.

O divine Master, grant that I may not so much seek
to be consoled as to console,
to be understood as to understand,
to be loved as to love.
For it is in giving that we receive,
it is in pardoning that we are pardoned,
and it is in dying that we are born to eternal life.
Amen."

CHANGE AND INTEGRATION SUMMARY

Change is a necessity of life. It is a natural evolution for our soul growth that can be reflected by our immediate environment. Every part of nature goes through some form of change process. Nature does not resist; it just is, and we cannot begin to become resistant to its calling when it is being asked from us. Change isn't easy, but if we muster up the courage to forgive and do actions which we know are right for us, then we open up our heart and life to the blessings that life has to offer.

If you don't change and allow integration you may stay stuck in the cycle of the same lessons, same circumstances and it becomes the reason why negative emotions come up because it is just providing you feedback from your soul that something isn't congruent with your alignment. It's rising in you. You are being called and you can no longer live in an inauthentic way. The way of the Spirit is coming through. The Truth of your Light, love and being.

Your breakthrough comes from your commitment to transcend the old into the magical you which has existed within you all along. All that was changed was that which clouded you from seeing this magnificent part of you. Welcome your transcendence. It is the integration of a newly defined you.

PART V
TRANSCENDENCE

You can't look back now when a new identity has emerged

The root of suffering is attachment.
— BUDDHA

SIMPLICITY

Some people think that the way to enlightenment is complicated, yet the answer is actually quite simple—simplify your life. As I stripped away my ego, my spirit began to whisper my deepest wishes. Our spiritual journey asks us to release our materialistic attachments and fear-based constructs of life, to come into deep surrender and receptivity to the flow of life. Simple thoughts, simple actions. Spirit is just simple. It's through the simplicity are we able to experience peace, bliss and Spirit. We are actually designed to be simple beings.

When we feel off-centre and our life feels crazy, we are living more of the world than of our Spirit. Take things off your to-do list. Reconnect with Spirit. We are a society that glorifies multi-tasking. However, multi-tasking takes us out of the present moment. Do one soulful activity for a substantial amount of time each day. If it means getting up a half hour earlier to go for that walk or meditating, do what you need to do to bring life back to simplicity. When we focus on the present, we bring the whole of us here in the now. That is the most powerful state of creation. What we learnt in the past has its place.

To begin to access more flow, direct your energy to receive more simplicity in life. Wanting more only makes us feel that we don't have enough. Then we over strive for more, that can taint our spirit and act out in ways that aren't attuned to our nature. We try to feel worthy or important by making our lives busy. Balance brings more flow. We can judge for not doing anything, but that is the cure to chaos that may be entering your life.

As I was looking to understand who I was in the world, I began to do so many courses, as well as aiming for leadership positions because I wanted the *label*. I didn't see how detrimental it became to my wellbeing. Slowly, I began to relinquish jobs or trying to keep myself busy. I soon noticed that my vitality increased. When I was at a job that asked me to do the impossible just because I had a label I knew it wasn't the life I wanted to live. I craved simplicity. As I stripped away anything that was unnecessary. I found so much peace in my life. I strived for more of this. I was still willing to work hard, but I didn't want to live my life in chaos anymore. The mental, emotional and physical strain wasn't worth it. Having energy to spend on the things I loved was what mattered most. I set an intention that I would simplify my life and only choose actions that brought more peace in my life. Over complicating your life is a sign that you're running from the ego. Choosing to simplify your life is a sign you're operating from Spirit. Live as if each day you're choosing to live like you're at a serene place that expands your heart.

**Be content where you are.
Be content with who you are.
In every moment, we already have more than enough.**

> **SOUL MASTERY LESSON**
> * Align your thoughts and actions to obtain peace.
> * Take one action step to simplify your life every day.
> * If something becomes too complicated or you're feeling overwhelmed, it's time to strip back into simplicity.
> * Simplifying your life helps to revitalise your spirit.

SPIRITED LIFE

All events are leading you to live an inspired life. To live in Spirit. True inspiration comes from the flow of the Universe. In an inspired state of being you have more energy and life feels effortless. Why is it that people can walk on coal in an inspired state and not feel a thing? Is this some magic voodoo or is there some magic when the mind and your physiology are in an inspired state?

I strive to be inspired. It feels like it's the language of the soul. A feeling that only generates more magnetic and positive feelings, experiences and thought processes. It's as if a veil becomes lifted and your awareness expands. Intuitive insights have a greater potential to be felt and heard in an inspired state. If you've been seeking guidance this is the state to aim for. You are Spirit. In an inspired state, fear has no place. You can understand that everything and anything is possible.

Tune in to those who in this moment provide the greatest inspiration for you. They offer the opportunity to open your heart deeper and show the way for you to access your heart's potential. In the past, the ancients inspired each other. They aimed, through adversity, to bring about messages of hope which activated faith. Inspiration is one feeling we should truly aim to be aligned to. It's our true divine unlimited potential activated. It generates an energy that can only be described as extraordinary and magical.

Feeling inspired actually helped me to get through even the most difficult times. It keeps your energy high-vibe and moves stagnant energy quickly. People ask me, how are you so happy all the time? It's not that I am happy all the time. The difference is that I consciously choose to feel good wherever I show up. If I'm not in an inspired state, I know that I'm not truly my best Self. Inspiration gets our mindset in the right place and helps us to stay strong in our heart centre.

If you're wanting to do anything creative or wanting to embark on something new, getting in an inspired state is the best energy that you can create from. People will feel—whatever you're co-creating with the Universe—that it feels good. With every inspirational idea that comes to your mind, remember to say, 'Thank you for this.' Each and every time, a spark of energy is overflowing your cup so that you can feel the nourishment that being in Spirit offers.

Soul time is pure flow. Time constraints doesn't exist. Being so immersed into an inspired state of consciousness brings that feeling of effortless flow with energetic potency. Time can fly by without us understanding where it went. You are living the flow of your soul.

SOUL MASTERY INQUIRY

* What inspires you and makes your heart become filled with love?
* Who inspires you?
* Think of a time when you have been in a state where time has

felt non-existent and you were so immersed in a task because you were in love with it.
* An inspired state opens the possibility for miracles.
* Sometimes others or circumstances will occur to open your heart to help to help get you in a state of inspiration.
* Inspirations helps to give you a spark, makes your energy high vibe and keeps your sacred container flowing.

YOUR SACRED GIFTS

For so many years I didn't know what I was good at. Especially after my awakening. I was searching for a job that would reflect what I loved but often I never felt like I wasn't good enough at any of the jobs that I could see myself potentially doing. Even when I went into a job that had the title where I thought I'd find fulfillment; it didn't eventuate that way. I saw people thriving and I compared myself to them because I did so much training. *Why wasn't I as talented as them, they're doing the same thing as me?* I did training to try and fit in a box of what I thought I needed to become. I worked part-time doing energy healing whilst teaching. I thought that maybe I'd do energy healing for the rest of my life because I saw others with the same gift and thought that's what I was meant to do and that I would eventually phase out of teaching. Then I thought about becoming a psychic reader. I knew I had a gift, but that didn't feel right also to just be that.

It was beginning to feel like I was Goldilocks trying to find what was right but never could. It was incredibly frustrating. I learnt many healing modalities and then started to venture into coaching, thinking that this could possibly be the way I wanted to go. I had always loved nutrition and when the Integrative Institute of Nutrition Health Coaching course came along, I was excited because I always had an interest in health, especially nutrition. Many of the people I looked up to along the way had done this course too so maybe I would become exactly like them.

If you idolize others, you can lose your identity following someone else's dream. It's why it's better to follow your own way. I picked up great strategies and it was truly one of the best courses I had ever done in my life, but again, I didn't want to box myself in being a coach either. It felt like there was a lot of them out there and how could I measure up to what they were doing? I didn't feel it was all that I was meant to do. With so much training, what was I meant to do? No 'job' title gave me the that soulful satisfaction and I was still striving for more. When we strive for more, we are often saying, 'I need this, whatever it is (for me it was my courses that I did) to validate myself.' You can't see what's right in front of you, your blessings and gifts that you have within you now.

One day out of the blue I had an epiphany. I chose to change my perception. *What was I good at?* I was good at listening, teaching, inspiring, helping, finding the humour in things, making circumstances feel lighter and transforming people's perceptions and lives was something that had always come naturally for me. I was inspired by topics about health, fitness, transforming thoughts and perceptions, and truly divine wisdom. I was always great with words and had deep insights. I always had the ability to see things beyond what others could see. I began to see the impact I made by just being me. It wasn't about the 'title' that I had, but how much of me I could bring. I knew that if someone was down at work, I could bring them up to feel better. If I sat in an office as a psychologist, I wouldn't be able to help others like that. It's all those incidental moments that count. Some of you may be destined for a big career and some of you may feel content with what you are and where you are, whatever it is, is right for your soul development. As I understood more of who I was my purpose began to find me. It inspired me to write and get out into the world to make a difference.

Wherever I was, I brought my whole toolkit of gifts and I don't box myself to say, this is only what I'll ever be. Maybe there's a reason why I have 'Jac' in my name, why not be a 'jack of all trades' and still gain mastery. I'm so grateful for all the training I have felt compelled to do because I picked up on valuable strategies that gave me an understanding on what I like or what doesn't fit me. A certificate gives the world an understanding what you've done, but it's your actions that will define the true impact that you can make. You know what you're meant to do because you just seem to be at the right place, at the right time, wherever you show up. The clients come when you're doing the work. Even the clients you have a soul contract with will show up because you've organised long ago that this is what you're here to do. I got into teaching because of my family, because that was what I was preconditioned to believe. That it was a good job and what I was meant to do. My sister was a teacher, why not me? I mean it's not a bad job. Teaching taught me a lot and it was in my Soul Blueprint to do so. I had to be there because it helped me to learn how to structure lessons that are now used as workshops. I could see the next wave of souls come through and how they are going to need a lot of guidance to navigate through this next wave in humanity. For me, it ignited the passion to not only help kids but adults as well. When I began to own my ability to help others, I found that I was able to help more people and I would be given circumstances that I knew I could handle so that others could heal.

My awakening made me judge myself too. Why had I wasted all this time and only just awakened now? I wanted to get out and do everything because this wasn't the life that I had chosen. I started off with the life chosen by my family. However, I realised I was there for a reason. My gifts were being utilised. When I shifted my perception, I can't tell you all of the blessings that I received and how I shifted out of spaces that weren't soulful. Your life will reflect where your state of being is. Everything you experience is purposeful and the Divine is working and flowing with you. Your awakening will push you to your next step.

As you strip your identity, you can easily lose your sense of Self. It can even get down to doubting what are you good at and where your life is heading. Your deeper search for the meaning of where you fit in this world can go into deep reflection that might leave you more confused than with certain clarity. Your life has not been a waste. In deep emotional processes, you can throw your hands up in the air and think, *I'm not good at anything! What is my purpose? What can I do in my life that will be meaningful?* What you enjoy or find effortless doesn't need to change because you have a new awareness opened up to you. You are beginning to learn how you can use your talents with your expanded awareness. Also, with experience, new talents and gifts will emerge. Every single person on this planet has some form of gifts and talent. It might mean asking others what they see you do effortlessly. It might be that you're great at listening to others, cooking, cleaning, teaching, handling finances, and even organising.

Own what you're good at. As you hone in on the things which you're great at, they become even stronger. We can focus on the deficits, but this is why we have others who exhibit the deficits because that's their gift! If you're a great listener, it doesn't mean you'll end up being a psychologist, but it could be a pathway which you look at for the future. It might just mean that in whatever organisation of work you're in they need someone to be there to help others to heal. We are placed perfectly wherever we need to be.

You may wish to do some professional development along the way which will help you to hone further into your skillset. Maybe you've always dreamed of being a naturopath but feel your time is up, it never is. Your dreams that reflect your interests can always become self-actualised if you put your mind to it. The only thing standing in your way is you.

You never know when your talents will pop-up in extraordinary circumstances to receive some form of fulfillment. We might have an idea of a job that uses our interests, but it can come in other unconventional ways because we need to learn other skills in order to fill out our divine plan. When I was working at a school, halfway throughout the year we had a new sport teacher come in and it was with the sport teacher that I had to collaborate with and do some jobs around the school. One of the jobs that we were required to do was work in the garden. The sport teacher was so excited because he loved the garden. Earlier on in his life, he had always wanted to become a horticulturist and loved gardening. On a side note, lucky for me that he came around because I had no idea about gardening although I learnt along the way! Although the workplace environment was slightly toxic, he found so much fulfillment being in the garden and in an unconventional way he was living out his dream working in the garden. It was his escape and it opened up his heart. In a strange way for me too, working in the garden ignited my passion for healing with the earth.

My grandparents owned a very successful farm in their day. It was in my DNA. When I worked in the garden, I felt the presence of my grandmother and my ancestors helping me to access the gifts that they brought into their incarnation. Although, I came in only knowing how to weed, I embraced the potential that the challenge brought. If you are in a circumstance that can be challenging, if you're willing to persist there may be a new skill, gift or learning that's waiting to unveil. It took me about eight months to truly see the transformation that slowly became something I became passionate about. I even started growing my own organic fruits, vegetables and herbs because I wanted to be light and have my life be an expression of the Light.

> **Your soul seeks growth, allow it to flourish.**
> **Give yourself some credit for how gifted you truly are!**

Don't be stuck on the idea that you are a certain identity or have fixed likes. When you bring your expanded awareness into each and every moment, you allow more opportunities for your strengths to become stronger and other gifts to filter through in your life. You are already expressing your talents and gifts and it is supporting you now to fulfil your divine purpose. You are already doing it. You have to be willing to see your goodness.

SOUL MASTERY INQUIRY

* If you are unsure of your gifts and talents, ask a close friend to tell you what are you great at?
* We are in the right place, at the right time, so that we can discover our gifts and talents or move towards experiences that allow our gifts to shine.

* What gifts are you doing effortlessly every day?
* What is one positive thing that you bring each day to yourself, to someone else and the world?
* What skill have you noticed change into a gift or talent over time?
* What is grabbing your interest now to upskill and evolve?
* You might *not* know exactly what 'job' you're meant to do but see the value you bring to your life as well as others each and every day.
* Your identity needs to be stripped so you can see the blessing that you are.

INTEGRITY

When someone's actions or words aren't in alignment or integrity, you will feel that stirring within. This is the transcendence of authenticity. In the beginning, we are discovering the authenticity of our soul. As we continue to unveil the aspects of our soul, we can't help but live in integrity which is the alignment of your mind, emotions, body and spirit.

If someone or an organisation you feel no longer aligns with your values, release them. Being in integrity, living your word and acting in your truth is what sets you up to live out your purpose. Integrity is becoming accountable for your words and actions, knowing that it has to resonate with your being. If others or experiences are not expressing what your perceived truth is, then have the courage to release them. You are being presented with an illusion, stand in your truth and claim your soul power. If you act out of a lack of integrity, you are giving your power away. It's through the actions of integrity that you can begin to realise how powerful you truly are. You can feel the alignment of your soul being present in your life. Honour yourself and acknowledge how far you've come.

MEAN WHAT YOU SAY.

ACT ACCORDINGLY TO YOUR SOUL.

HONOUR YOUR JOURNEY

One summer afternoon I started crying. I was triggered by the feeling of rejection that I was left out of a group date. As I was crying, I noticed that I had a new level of awareness and I checked in. I realised that I actually wasn't upset because I shouldn't have been invited to this event anyway. There was a part of me releasing old habits and paradigms. It was a strange feeling. On a mental layer when I checked in, I was okay with this. On an emotional layer, I wasn't upset with what was happening, so, why was I crying? There was a part of my physical layer that was holding onto the rejection, deeply seated. I saw this was an opportunity that a part of my old paradigm was releasing, so a new way could occur. As you move deeper into your awareness, you'll begin to notice that sometimes these moments of crying sporadically is just a process of old wounds healing. I felt relieved in that moment that the hard work I had been doing for so long was finally resolving itself, even if it took time for all parts of my being to catch up. There will be times when emotions will hit you out of the blue. Deep processes will come up. With a new heightened level of awareness, you will come to a state of deep wisdom to shift it. Honour where you are at. Acknowledge the great work you have put in to even get to this level of awareness and detachment of the ego's construct. Allow yourself to let go completely.

When we have been working through one thing after another, we may not get a chance to say thank you to all our good work and the good things that have happened for us. Taking a moment in gratitude can help shift a positive momentum in your favour. If you forget to take time out and acknowledge the hustle you've done for your soul growth, you may get stuck in an emotional down spiral. You wouldn't be here right now without all the great work you've done.

SOUL MASTERY INQUIRY

* What are my thoughts about what's happening?
* How do I feel about _____?
* What brought on this trigger?
* What event caused this?
* When was the last time I felt this way deeply?
* What is the wisdom it is trying to tell me?
* Compared to the past, how do you positively react now to this event?
* Give yourself a hi-five! Look how far you've come!

Allow yourself to cry or get physical.
Your intuitive feelings will guide you to the best way to shift this.

YOUR PHYSICAL BODY

Your physical body is a sacred vessel for you to carry out the work you are meant to do. Honouring your temple requires the dedication and commitment to your soul. Your soul can't do the work it's meant to do if you're not working! For your soul to illuminate in this sacred space we have to treat our physical body with the love and kindness it deserves.

When we open up to Spirit we work through the mental and emotional layers of our auric field. This causes us to be still. We need stillness to give the mind time to process whatever is happening. One part of the process you can neglect is the physical container that's trying to keep you altogether. The cells in your body need time to regenerate and if you're stuck in a deep process that has taken time for you to get over, this can cause you to feel sluggish and stuck. Depending on your habits, we may choose to cope with adversity through obsessive binge eating, going back to childhood eating patterns, drinking, or the use of other types of addictive substances, or not physically moving. There has to be a balance between soothing and numbing.

It is particularly important that when you are feeling really stuck that you *do* move. Movement will help support the other layers of your being and give an opportunity for your soul to shine through. Gentle movements may include yoga or a walk. Maybe start with some yoga poses when you wake up if you physically don't feel like getting out of bed. The more you 'support' your body through fitness and nutrition, the stronger you're able to cope with things, as you regenerate the cells in your body to be the 'new you'. This is what you do want.

The deep awareness you receive on your processes are there for you to release. Sometimes, these vibrations can be sticky to our being. Your Higher Self has brought this to your attention because it wants to let it go. It knows that it no longer serves you anymore. We have to be willing to let it go. If there's a part of us that wants to hold onto it or is finding it hard to let go, we have to physically let it go and assist our physical body and mind through reprogramming.

On Earth, we are bound by cycles and rhythms. The flow of nature. Nature gives us clues on exactly how to navigate through life. Nature is the only process that can't be controlled my humankind, unless it gets compromised. Here the Divine speaks to us each day, reminding us how we should live. Our physical body isn't dissimilar to nature. We all have rhythms we depend on. It's the nature of our being and it is our genetic makeup. Sleep, menstruating, eating patterns, these are just some examples on how we are affected by the rhythm of our body. Constant exposure to limiting beliefs and thoughts or if we are around negative people, their thoughts become ours as they transfer into our subconscious mind and these are also rhythmic patterns of the mind.

This is why nurturing your mind and body come hand in hand, as they will both influence your ability to be stable and become the driving force for you to be able to live out your destiny. Your body is the vehicle to step out into the world. When your mental state isn't the best, it's your divine will that's in conjunction with your physical body that can help shift your state quicker. Even when you find it hard to get out of bed, go out for a walk. Push yourself to move when you feel like you've been drowning in your emotions and negative thought patterns for too long. You have to help yourself. No-one can control the way you think or make you move other than yourself. You are in the driving seat. This is why it's a two-way process. Your Higher Self will open the gateway to your healing, but you still have to do the work as it is in your sacred contract that you came here to work through. You can do it. Deep down, in the seat of your soul, you know that all processes are leading you to more joy in your life which is the nature of your soul essence. It is your birthright.

Sometimes the most 'spiritual' act you can do is be a muggle and enjoy muggle things. A spiritual muggle. If you haven't seen Harry Potter, a muggle is someone who is a human and does not possess magical gifts like a wizard. You may need to cut down meditation time to move. Your physical body is what helps to integrate your soul into humanity. So, enjoy doing muggle things that physically ground you back into feeling more like yourself again.

SOUL MASTERY LESSON

* When you're feeling stuck, move.
* Nurture your physical body.
* Your physical body will always support you and work with your soul, even when your mind says it can't.
* Moving your physical body will help shift your process quicker

and help you to move on.

* Regenerate your cells: through drinking lots of water, using affirmation, body movements, meditation. Rhythmic patterns engage a new consciousness that filters through your being.

EXPANDED CONSCIOUSNESS

I felt I was in a void period for quite some time, yet there wasn't a doubt in my mind that I was in the right place, at the right time. I knew the next phase of my life was not yet ready, and I had to be in a space where I was still growing, yet it fulfilled me on some level. It was also in this state that I began to feel lost. As it felt there was no momentum going forward. I had gone back into feeling more 'human' than ever before. I was feeling off-centre. I was trying to go back to my rituals that help activate my heart space, but nothing seemed to be working. I had forgotten an aspect of my true Self, my divine nature. Nothing was inspiring me. Everything was boring. I felt dull, as if someone had switched off the light switch in my heart. I thought enough was enough and decided to act. It wasn't until I went in for a healing that I began to remember a part of me that I didn't realise I was missing. As I closed my eyes, I could feel myself amongst the stars. A sense of oneness and an overwhelming feeling of unconditional love entered into every cell of my being. I felt home again. Like being hit with amnesia, throughout all the processes of letting go, I had forgotten 'me'.

There comes a time when we realise that life is not just about us. There is a deeper aspect of ourselves that reaches beyond our thoughts, feelings and perceptions. An expanded awareness of consciousness. How can you describe this expansion other than the feeling of the soul in its full potentiality? The more we let go of, the lighter we become. As we have worked hard and what feels endless to release the confinements of our personality to reach our divine Self. Our true identity. It's in this state we can uncover our true purpose in life. It's in this state we can understand the paradoxical nature of separation and oneness. The ultimate perception of an unlimited divine being living a human experience.

The ascension process is about descension. The truth is that the higher we go in increasing our light body, the more grounding we have to do to bring it all down into this physical realm. That is the magic, the mystical, in its full manifestation.

When the Universe asks you to move forward with faith, take the leap.

Each test of faith that you overcome allows the illusion of control to dissolve. The controlling aspect that restricts you from moving forward. If it feels like it's breaking you, it means that Spirit has broken through. Another old condition is transforming. Another flow of blessings is coming your way.

SPIRITUAL INFLUENCER

You are gifted with the assignment to be a spiritual influencer. This isn't the notion of you placing what you believe onto others. It's being in a state of being your authentic Self that allows for people to shift in your space. A place where you allow others to grow. When you've awakened to a greater sense of Self and aligned with your life purpose, you are automatically put into places where you can create the greatest influence. This space *must* come from the space of Spirit. Anything else would mean you'd be a spiritual ego influencer, rather than just allowing Spirit to work through you. When you can impact someone's life, even if it's just one person, including your own, you can be self-assured that the Universe is working with you to help shift the consciousness of this planet. If you have the capacity to change lives, do so.

Being authentically aligned with your true Self will create the influence that's required. There is *no* force, only flow. People new to the path and those who've been around for a while will see your growth and progress and you will act as a guardian to assist their growth. You can help assist them to see the Light in their heart, their path and see the 'truth'.

EVERY WORD AND ACTION YOU TAKE, MAY IT ALWAYS COME FROM THE RIGHT PLACE.

LIFE PURPOSE

Your life purpose—the moments that you feel have the most meaning—unfolds sporadically. Your life purpose happens to you. Your life purpose presents itself in how much of you, you decide to discover and own. When you know with conviction what you're meant to do in this present moment—presence is the key—then go and do that. Your 'ultimate purpose' is not a destination but about how you live each little moment that led you to live your life's calling. You will have grand moments of achievement which should be celebrated. If you hold your expectations of fulfillment through only a grand achievement, you sell yourself short. Your impact is determined by what you do for yourself on a soul level which your mind could never comprehend or understand the enormity of transformation it has created.

> ### SOUL MASTERY INQUIRY
> * What has been some synchronistical moments where there has been clarity given for your next steps?
> * What have you done in the past week that has been intentional and purposeful for yourself or another?

* How do you see your life purpose unfolding for you right now?

YOUR LIFE PURPOSE IS MANIFESTING MAGICALLY IN THIS PRESENT MOMENT.

BALANCING ENERGIES

Diving into your sacred journey, your divine feminine unlocks the gateway to your awakening. Your divine feminine is flow, feelings and magic. It's through the deep immersion of your beautiful sacred feminine that you are able to tap into the 'Divine' to help you fulfil your life purpose. Through the hard work of staying in the divine feminine you begin to capture and activate your soul gifts. Your intuition naturally becomes much stronger as you work with the flow of the Universe. Your body and Spirit become one. The divine feminine also makes you face things that aren't of the heart. This is where we may have experienced many mental and emotional processes and you can feel you've been in the deep womb of the mother for a long time. People can focus purely too much on the feminine or the masculine. Feminine is receptive, whereas the masculine is action orientated. The divine masculine is forward momentum.

When it comes to our life purpose, we can access the answers to whatever we need by balancing the feminine aspect within us. This is where you can receive the guidance and insight that you need in order to move forward. The mother knows what's possible for creation in the materialistic world, hence it is a very powerful energy. However, it's balancing the masculine aspect of our being that allows the seed of creation to come to life. The more we have been awakened to a new life; we can easily get stuck in our processes that keep us stuck. Too much immersion in both worlds equals no equilibrium and conscious creation. As you move away from toxic people or circumstances it's easy to get stuck in the hurt and pain of what's happened to us. That's where we need to talk about the divine masculine. When you haven't felt supported, our masculine can feel shot and your feminine aspect can become mistrusting, leading you to retreat into the comfort of the feminine.

The solar plexus—our power centre—also greatly associated with masculine energy need a power up. Without a balance in both feminine and masculine energy, we are unable to have the vitality we need to live our purpose. The masculine is the Divine Creator to make all things possible. Slowly and surely, allow yourself to be supported by others. Take a leap of faith to act on a creative idea that you've had in meditation. Get physical so that your body supports your mental and emotional body. This can help you to rise out of anything you're going through. We can never focus on just one side of the equation because that just brings about extreme polarity. If we are too much in our feminine, we are emotional beings. If we are too much in our masculine, we exert our power and can risk operating from the world of the mind.

SOUL MASTERY INQUIRY

* Tune into your energy right now. Are you too much in your masculine or feminine? The feminine feels passive and the masculine is forceful.
* What type of energy does your soul need to be in today?
* What can you do to stay balanced, centered and aligned?

WHO AM I?

In a sea that's motionless, not knowing where your ship will sail, the constant ebbs and flows leaves a distinct feeling of hope that somehow you will get to your destination. The uncertainty of how long it will take you to get there or what might present itself is common for this journey we undertake. We can assume that the ship will have smooth sailing from weather reports, but the weather can change instantly, and we can experience some unexpected sea troubles as it changes your path completely. A path that might have seemed safer to go through, takes a turn and you may go another way due to the external conditions. You may get lost and have to decide to use a guide to assist you on the way. We can either be affected by the external conditions that presents itself, or we can stay true to course because we know what our destination is, our true Self.

Knowing who you are is a constant evolutionary process. When we've learnt who to be and then become awakened, we have to learn to search for who we truly are. The constant seeking for the meaning of life and who you are can make you feel fatigued if you're looking externally for the answers. What are we really searching for? When all is lost, who is your guiding light? I felt completely lost and had lost faith in what I saw around me. I worked on my perceptions and my habits, but I was still surrounded by corruption, darkness and things that caused me to give up on this world. Through all this awakening process, what was the point? What was the point if I was still going to experience pain and suffering? What good was it to try and do affirmations everyday if I still saw the same things happen? On a side note before I continue: I do believe we are co-creators of our reality, but there are parts where you just know you did not attract certain circumstances in your life due to your thoughts. There is not an ounce of your subconscious mind that created this existence and I think it has to be made clear—especially as it is a sensitive issue with people who have been inflicted with some form of traumatic event—we might not even have that level of understanding until we leave this existence. We might not know the reason why we had to go through that pain. Don't let the story make you a victim of life but find that inner strength to rise from whatever it is that keeps you small.

There was a period of time where I couldn't find satisfaction in the things I valued most or what gave me joy. I had stripped so much of my identity that I couldn't find the joy in my relationships; work, and I felt no creativity. I was really upset with Spirit because I'd worked so hard to get to where I was, to heal many aspects of myself, know myself deeper, doing what I felt was required and asked of Spirit. However, when I reflected in my life what I wanted to feel or what I wanted to achieve, it just felt I was dipping into a black hole of uninspired action. And even saying that makes me feel like I had a big gaping hole in my heart. To everyone, I can easily adapt to what they need so they weren't able to see the suffering I was experiencing inside.

For me, the greatest pleasure is to feel inspired. Heart expanded openness that feels like the grace of God flows through you. I experienced this state so many times. No matter what I did or what avenues I chose I couldn't find that which lit me up inside as I had felt a few years before. I looked around and again I was outraged and disgusted on the same boring content on social media. The world felt small. I was let down by people around me and even to those who I looked up to, disappointed. I had lost the feeling of Oneness again and that sense of connection of all living things to the Divine. I was meditating, doing all those spiritual things, working on my physical body—eating, fitness, mindset—I just couldn't understand what more I could actually do to know myself, as well as free my mind and body from the confinements of Earth. I felt really out of place. I thought differently. I felt differently. I could easily talk and gossip to others to connect, but it wasn't a conversation that fulfilled me. I had *lost all* fulfillment in life.

So, like someone grasping for survival, I again searched for the meaning of life. I knew that there's only a few people who actually inspire me and helped me get into my heart. And again, it was my trusted, dear teacher, Dr Wayne Dyer, who never seems to fail. I was listening to another inspirational speaker who spoke about how she would ask the Spirit of Wayne Dyer to be present with her before every talk. She talked about his Spirit being around us if we call upon it. For me, I know that deep within my heart, he's still helping millions on the other side of the ethers. When I heard this, I started to pray. I asked Wayne and my Spirit team to help guide me on the path to wisdom and inspiration. This is one of the greatest acts of love you can give to the world. A few days later, I began to remember a workshop that I had attended of his. I admired how he would seek the wisdom of the ancients and would translate this into our current world today. For every book he mentioned, I made sure to get it somehow. The thought popped into my head about how he had studied the words of Jesus and Lao-Tzu and how they were similar in their messages. I remember that I had downloaded it on my Kindle, so I began to read. As I did, my heart started to fill up. I decided to not read the interpretation of the authors take on the passages. I wanted to feel the living embodiment of what each word and energy was saying. I had a sense of deeper understanding that there might've been the possibility that Wayne used these ancient teachings into his own healing and quest for the deeper meaning of life. Clues are given through his work. The teachings that he put into his books act as a gateway, a quest for you to find your own navigation system.

For so long, I had used inspirational speakers for the answers to the Divine. Once I knew everything in terms of the content that they had delivered I knew it wasn't enough. Our clues are given by the ancient ones, as those who best experienced the Divine could only express a part of it. That's why we probably have different religions—one cause—yet different philosophies. When we culminate as a society, an Earth tribe, we will be able to see that what we seek, the Divine is finding all the avenues it can to get to you. It will present itself in any channel. This was now my time to go inward. To put into words the Divine, it can't be done. It's through the continual stripping of the ego, being of service and being our best and present Self, is what will change the world. Our purpose in life is more than to merely exist, it is to find 'who we are' in the reflection of the Divine and how this Divine would manifest in a world that's built on false illusions. Bring your best divine Self in all situations, and you will begin to see your life unfold.

What is your Divine identity?
Your true identity is to serve.

**Unveil your soul presence to the world and it will serve the world greatly.
Unveil your true identity to the world and it will serve the world greatly.**

When you've been stripped away—naked and bare—go where it excites you, no matter how mundane it might seem.

UNIVERSAL SPIRIT

We originate from a spark of Source. This spark becomes divided into parallel Universes, expressing itself trying to find that sense of wholeness. On another level, particular aspects of our reality assist us in helping us to remember our true form. It opens our heart and mind that there is a presence at play which we may desire to label but we just can't find the right words to describe it. We are tuning in, connecting and feeling into the cosmos.

In each person we feel attracted to something, whether it's the angels, elementals, consciousness, galactic, science and other principles that give them a greater understanding on the meaning of life. This is because on their energetic blueprint, this is the best way for them to find their true Self and bring alignment to their highest purpose. None can be dismissed as wrong.

Each part is an extension of Source. There have been times when I only believed in just the angels. This morphed and changed as I moved through my journey. What is out there is beyond our comprehension, yet there is still simplicity in the Universal Spirit that resides in and all around us.

SOUL MASTERY INQUIRY

* What brings you the greatest connection to the Universal Spirit?
* What is the best way in which you express this?

HIGH-VIBE COMMITMENTS

As the lessons pass through you with a heightened awareness, you'll come to a point where you realise it's not what you know, it's what you do and how you connect with your heart. Being unplugged from the matrix of life, you begin to vibrate at a higher frequency because you're consciously choosing to feel positive vibrations such as love, gratitude and peace which are 'lighter' in frequency.

When you feel stuck in denser emotions or are not doing what feels authentic for your soul, you can feel it within your being. Your feedback system on a physical, mental and emotional becomes more transparent as your spiritual layer, intuition increases. Once you awaken, you can only be aligned to higher vibrational commitments for your soul. It doesn't mean you won't experience any pain, the pain that you experience becomes an indication what needs to be let go of in your life.

There is a big shift that happens in your heart. It pulls on your integrity and you can only act in a way that uplifts you, rather than drags you down. What high-vibe commitments do you make for your soul each day? What does it look like? Anything that expands your heart, grows your soul and makes you feel good on the inside. These are non-negotiables that keep you on track, build up your strength and makes you live your purpose each day. You may wish to begin by writing three high-vibe commitments that are non-negotiable for you daily. When you're clear about what makes you feel high vibe, then you're able to discern what might make you feel low vibe, which is anything that brings down your energy or spirit. High vibe commitments help you to become intentional with how you live each and every moment and helps you to have enough energy doing what you love, rather than being drained from something that brings you misery! Do whatever gives you the good *feels*.

SOUL MASTERY INQUIRY

* What high vibe commitments are you dedicated to make daily?
* Get your journal out and split the page in half labelling it with two categories, 'High Vibe' and 'Low Vibe'. See what you commit to in your day. Whatever makes you feel lower in energy, put that in the low vibe column. Anything that makes you feel good put it in the high vibe. At the end of the day look at what you committed to. Is there something that you want to commit to more often? What is something in your low vibe column that can be changed?
* Your vibe is infectious. Choose the one that makes you feel uplifted.

HOW MAY I SERVE TODAY?

We are here to serve. To serve the collective conscious in helping them to open up their awareness in some shape or form. We are the make-shifters to help come from the space of the ego, to the presence of the divine heart where we live out our highest calling and potentiality. We are alike in Source's image as we are a creator of our experience. We are limited in our human form to our capacity for true freedom of the Spirit and what or how long it may take to create. You may not be an Oprah and you may not want that lifestyle anyway. What matters is what you do in each moment that helps others in some form or capacity. Acknowledge the part of yourself that helps others, it's not always about just giving to charity if it comes from an empty heart, although every donation you make counts.

Ask, what is it in your job or your role at home or social situations that lights up others in some shape or form? When you begin to recognise these moments—the moments where you rock up at the right place, at the right time, or make someone smile—feel into your heart expanding and know that you allowed the Divine to work through you, in that moment. That moment where you allowed peace to flow through instead of hate. That moment where your conversation, hug or space provided an opportunity for karma to shift for yourself and the other individual.

Unlock your destiny and say to the Universe,
"I am ready to be of service for you. Please put me in the right places at the right to and allow me to be the purest vessel for your divine work."

This is how we change the world.
One step at a time.
By being in the divine presence of your soul.
And so it is.

UNLEASH YOUR DESTINY

Unlocking your destiny is such an exciting process. Tap into the flow of the 'I AM presence'. You cannot *unfollow* your path as long as you're aligned to the calling of your divine destiny. Spirit will just show up for you and provide you what you need.

I've never liked the sound of our life as just an experiment, but we should treat it this way. If we can have the courage to take the risks and see the rewards of our trust in a greater presence, life becomes much more meaningful. We don't test the Universe, as the Universe provides all that we truly need. We stop feeling the flow when we try and go against the current, rather than going with the divine plan that will reward us abundantly. It's like the Universe is saying, 'Hello there! I know a greater plan for you, roll with me.'

Surrender is the most *loved* and *disliked* word on this journey. If you can put up with the rhythm of the Universe, you can expect to live out the highest calling of your soul. If you experienced enlightenment straight away, your mind would not be able to cope with its environment, or the truth that there is simplicity, love, peace, contentedness, flow and magic when you search deep down for the answer. From an ego's perspective, these simple truths don't seem complex enough. The Ego asks, *shouldn't it be more complicated?*

When we surrender to peace and acceptance, everything else just feels like flow. Love enters the space of the heart. Lightness of heart. Our essence feels lighter and brighter. Surrendering becomes easier when we have learnt how to trust, and it is here that we can just surrender into our purpose without having to do a thing but be ourselves.

YOUR SOUL CALL

There comes a time when the calling of your soul becomes louder than a whisper. At the start of your journey, you were trying to decipher and hear the guidance of your Higher Self. Here, the whispers were hard to hear but you followed the crumbs, the clues, that helped you to get you to where you now. But something miraculous happens when you're on a soul journey. There comes a time where you can no longer hide in your spiritual closet. The ego loses the ability to keep making excuses as to why you can't achieve each and every heart desire.

The illusion of what is impossible lifts. Your mind, body and soul integrate with each other to help you take that leap of faith. All you need to do to be in alignment is take that first step. Each step lights up your path. When you follow what lights you up, the path will light up for you to follow. If you only knew how powerful you are on a soul level, you'd never fear taking that step. Whatever you want to do, do it, regardless of fear. You must live a spirited life. It is normal that through each threshold and every decision you make, you may lose people in your life if they're not interested in what's best for you. The deeper you go, there can be more pain that unveils but you've come this far to know how to navigate through these sticky emotions that are ready to be transcended. When you submerge yourself into the deepest depths of the water, you come back up to the surface—cleansed, refreshed, initiated.

Inhaling a new breath of life. In this new life, invite joy in. If you don't like where you are submerged deeply, don't stay too long, rise to the surface, again and again. The great part about life is that we always have a chance for new beginnings. A choice for change.

What is possible is illuminated for you. The perceived conditions that held you back become transcended. Every time a condition holds you back, bring your awareness to the forefront. Your soul can transcend anything you desire. Pass it over to your Council of Light, your Spirit helpers, working together you're able to create the life that was orchestrated from your Soul Blueprint.

As your soul answers become loud, the ego voice becomes a distant part of your consciousness. You'll always receive the right guidance at the right time. The virtues of the soul become transparent and transfigures as your humanly essence. Patience becomes second nature as the cyclic rhythms of nature are understood.

GOOD THINGS COME TO THOSE WHO WAIT.

THE WORLD NEEDS YOU

What you bring to this world is special and unique. We are a gift to this world in every moment. Your role specifically for you, is what this world needs. That's why you chose to reincarnate. To spread your divine Self just the way you are. You didn't work lifetimes to behave in someone else's values, actions or thoughts. When we realise that just being us is the best gift we can give to the world, we become our divine Self. You're not above anyone else, you play such a pivotal role and ensuring that for you and others, the Divine is present in every moment. Through you, an expression of the Divine can manifest.

You've trained many lifetimes to come into this moment of time. There's no coincidence that more people are awakening, remembering and actioning their calling, even if they don't have full comprehension on what it might actually be. Our gifts help to transcend the old paradigms, the paradigms that are no longer relevant for the next wave of consciousness. We have to rise, rise higher than we have ever before. Even if pain exists within us, or we might be bound by circumstance temporarily, we can never give up on our important mission on coming into this existence.

YOU'RE A FOREVER BLOOMING FLOWER, BECOMING RICHER, EXPANSIVE, SEEKING THE SUN AND THE LIGHT OF YOUR SOUL.

KNOW THAT YOU ARE PERFECT JUST THE WAY YOU ARE. RIGHT WHERE YOU ARE NOW.

MATCH YOUR INTENTION

We have to train new neurological pathways to match our frequency and alignment to joy. This happens every time we choose to do something that is out of the norm. Our neurological pathways become stronger when we engage in a habit daily. Our physical actions can have an immense impact on our physiology. To change our state of mind, we have to change our physical state. This exercise, even though it might feel uncomfortable, can be a quick shift into lifting your vibration. Think about the joy of children. Children have a joy about them that is infectious. As a teacher, you could easily get them to laugh and smile through songs or getting them to move. It's time to move like you're at the best party of your life. It's time to see your life as a big party. Imagine waking up each day with that sort of energy?

As humans our brains are wired to overestimate how long it will take to get to our destination. Take a moment to imagine the goal you're working towards. Feel how happy you are achieving your goal. Now, put on some pumping music and celebrate. Put your arms in the air, jump up and down, a *woo-hoo* might even come into play, like youth at a party. You can do this with no-one watching or get some people to join you. I sometimes even do this when I'm in the car or no-one is home.

Celebrate standing up and sitting down, your physiology in both these stances are becoming trained to experience that light heartedness and positive energy coming through. This may sound crazy, but in order to get to where you want to be, you have to invite the frequency and momentum you need to move forward. Joy allows us to increase our stamina to complete anything we have our hearts set on. Our physical body is the vehicle for our journey. Why not make it fun?

> **SOUL MASTERY LESSON**
> * What sparks your joy?
> * Today consciously choose to bring joy wherever you go and in whatever you do.

YOU SHALL RECEIVE

When you align with joy, you begin to feel the difference in your energy. It's like the feeling after you've been sick and you're starting to feel vitality again. As you align with joy, you will begin to feel lighter. In this state, begin generating the energy you'd like to receive. Trusting in the Universe invites in a higher frequency flow to assimilate into your life. Trusting in the Universe can be one of the hardest things we do on our journey when we feel stuck. Redirecting your thoughts and energy to a higher vibration strengthens your pillar of strength and inner knowing. Visualizing what you'd like to receive and feeling what your visualizing is aligned to with your highest purpose aids with the flow of positive energy that is wanting and waiting to be generated into your life. This is an important part of the alignment process as all parts of your being catch up to be in full alignment.

You will receive signs along the way that you are making way. It might be even as simple as a knowing within your heart that you're on the right track. There's no explanation other than a comfort within that all is working in your favour. If your spiritual practice ramps up during this process, then you are working with the Universe to fine tune your human conceptual level of what your dreams are to your highest purpose. Your destiny then becomes inevitable. You may even meet people who act as a vessel of confirming what you're feeling. Some other signs include coins, feathers, repetitive numbers, waking up the same time, seeing words or objects that are confirmation for you that the Universe is letting you know the deliciousness of what is to come.

Alignment is a key to opening up our awareness, insight and perspective. With our super charged emotions out of the way, it helps us to gain strength to focus on what we need to focus on. Our energy becomes stronger when we have a clear focus on what we want. Our physical senses are heightened, because in a lighter frequency, you can follow the way with much more ease and grace.

When I learnt to let go and accept that I knew my path was unfolding the way it was meant to, my patience could see the unfolding and the signs of the Universe much more easily. It is as if you become more receptive to see the signs the Universe sends you, the little breadcrumbs—the signs, confirmations or pathways—that lead you to the gingerbread house—your dreams. Whenever you receive a confirmation or even if you haven't felt one yet, say thank you. Re-affirm in the power of this moment what you'd like to receive.

> *"Thank you, Universe, for aligning me on my path and showing me the way. I easily receive confirmations that I'm making the right choices for my life path and that every thought and action is aligned to my highest calling. Please continue to open my perspective to see through your eyes, so that the choices I make are for the highest good of all."*

Strengthen your faith in Spirit and Spirit will deliver. Our faith acts as a channel for the Universe to communicate what thoughts and actions we need to take. Learning to trust is a great lesson we will all encounter in our life. Spirit may not deliver in the way we think, but it doesn't mean they're not working for us. Spirit knows what is good and will always deliver what is best. Don't doubt the magic and power, the Universe will always pull through for you in your time of need.

THE POWER OF THE HEART

Even though emotions serve a purpose, they can become a super charged energy that overrides all aspects of your auric field. Sadness can make us feel stuck or it can slow the flow, stopping us from accessing our executive functioning centre which is one of the receptors for our intuitive guidance. Anger will overexert our energy. Fear will bring us to a complete standstill. In fear, we can lose ourselves to just merely existing. Each emotion—good or bad—act as responses that something needs to be in congruency with your heart and soul. Your whole energetic and genetic makeup has been created perfectly so that every experience that happens to you, is part of your divine destiny. Your whole human make up is amalgamated with the essence of your soul contract, which contains what needs to be cleared and transcended in this lifetime. It's through this physical reality that our awareness is brought to our attention and it's the physical evidence that can be shown that something is stirring within you by the reactions that you have on a physical, mental or emotional layer. All reactions are an indication that your soul is waiting for you to pay attention to something that is going on. As you continue to understand who you are, it's your job, just like a detective, to see what is not congruent with the soul.

Our emotions have the capacity to keep us off centre, creating a brain fog where we feel we can't receive the guidance we need to move forward. If there is an element of thought polarity, this brings emotional charge and intensity. Do what you know helps to balance *you*. Check in with your feelings. Stillness, wisdom and love is what will transcend most emotions.

When we understand our emotions from a higher perspective, our feedback mechanisms act as the alchemist to create the perfect blend of balance and restoration. Taking control of your life, restores your power. Your power to create any reality you desire. Ignore the signals from your being, the emotions become intensified. If you are truly aligned, you understand and feel no need to feel any other emotion other than love and gratitude.

Our struggle of polarities becomes less when we come into the strength of the heart. The heart is the gateway of the soul. Our soul presence is made manifested through each and every moment as love, gratitude and stillness generates flow, abundance and unconditional love in our life. When we come from the space of LEGS—Love, Energy, Gratitude and Stillness—we create the greatest change. Everything that happens in our life is because it comes from a higher intelligence. One that cannot be explained or questioned. Capture the moments where you feel this expansiveness. Your mind can access that memory to make it reality in the present. This is where our best decisions and actions can be made, reflecting your true Self.

With conviction, LEGS mean you are on purpose. Even the most challenging times come as a blessing from the Universe. The Universe is only acting to make life in complete harmony and balance. It's the ability to be in the true immersion of flow and Spirit. Making tracks with your LEGS.

> **SOUL MASTERY INQUIRY**
>
> To bring more LEGS in your day, ask:
> * How can I love more?
> * What brings me energy?
> * What am I grateful for?
> * How can I incorporate more stillness today?

THE ZERO POINT

Stillness will open the door to the Inner Self.

Every experience we have serves its purpose on the process of our evolution. If you're perceiving an event through an unauthentic positive emotion, this can be disguised as infatuation and can displace an imbalance of our energy. The Universe then conspires to create perfect harmony. Positive or negative, good or bad, these are charged polarities. To ensure we aren't experiencing the swing of the pendulum, we must come into the state of the Heart, The Zero Point. The Zero Point is at the centre, it is the cosmos manifesting in your heart centre. In this state, the only feeling is flow. Love, gratitude and contentedness coexist. The Zero Point is where Christ Consciousness flows through your heart. In this perspective, you view everything from a soul level. You see the benefits of a perceived negative experience. The positive side is acknowledged and simultaneously seen as serving a purpose. Here we enter the space of Unconditional Love, support, light and growth.

At the end of the Creation story, God saw everything was good and rested on the seventh day. God took time to appreciate everything that was created. There is a divine orchestration at play to bring you into a greater state of evolution. A greater state of empowerment. A greater ability to be the change agent that's needed to make this world a better place. The power of the heart is the most powerful aspect of human society that can transform the world. If everyone can come from the presence of the heart, balanced in their illusions, then imagine what kind of world we could have? Polarities are illusions because, in truth, everything is in balance in our life. When we experience good, we also experience bad simultaneously. When we choose to see both good and bad exist as one, as balanced, only then, can we be filled with love and gratitude in any moment. Your presence is your power.

SOUL MASTERY LESSON

* What brings you back into your presence?
* Bring back your focus to the now. This is your Empowered State.

THE NEXT STEP

Transcendence is opening the gateway for a new way of being. Your awareness, thoughts and actions are much more aligned to your soul and you can't think of being another way. Now, there are two possibilities that can occur. Your transcendence is moving you towards a self-actualised state which you may begin to feel a snippet of in your transcendental state of being. Here, you are learning how to self-actualise parts of your state of being. Mastering your life on a deeper soul level. Integrating your divine aspects into this physical realm. When we activate our self-actualised states of being, we are fully aligning our soul to our Highest Purpose and divine potentialities where all things are made possible. Activating our divine potential and living a life which feels right in the heart, connected and with purpose. These aspects activate our soul potential and will require great strength for it to evolve and transpire for you. For some, this will resonate with you, for others your path might be asking you to experience something completely different.

If you're going back into the cycle, it's because there's more learning that needs to be done to discover the beauty of your soul. To initiate and assist you in opening your eyes, mind and heart to see your divine aspects are made evident. This is the next step you may encounter. Entering back into the soul cycle to develop a new awareness of a lesson which may need to be transcended. New learning has to be made as part of an evolution of your soul. Know that you have enough tools to acknowledge and understand how to navigate better through the soul lessons that keep presenting itself. It's not bad to go back into the cycle, it's exactly what *you* need to experience right now for your soul's evolution.

Whatever path is needed is perfect for you. All roads are leading you towards the union of Source. If there's something that's blinding you from this happening, then it is a requirement of the soul to go back through the cycle and lift off another piece of illusion that keeps you separate from feeling anything other than goodness, magic and divinity.

TRANSCENDENCE SUMMARY

When you look back at your life and see yourself getting into the same circumstances and not reacting in the same way that you did, you know that you've transcended into a new way of being. It can feel as if all your entire system has had an upgrade and you're a completely different person because you have become someone that's truly living a life congruent with the soul. It's like a complete upgrade in your DNA, physiology, mindset and all your energetics. You know if you have transcended your lessons because when you are exposed to the same triggers or circumstances that once made you reactive, they now have no effect on you.

Through the gift of transcendence, you can begin to see that this isn't entirely about you but how you are integral in helping others. It is the gift of seeing things beyond the Self and what step you're making towards shifting the collective consciousness. If you've fully embodied a change, there's no choice but for things to shift within your immediate environment.

Not everyone will transcend their life lessons. Some will stay stuck in the cycle. Your transcendental state of being is showing you your self-actualised potentialities. It is aligning you to your divine potentials. It is showing you a snippet of your potential. Sometimes we may go back into the cycle because there's something else we may need to learn, a destined moment to be had and it might be an important point for us to be able to become self-actualised.

More and more, we are being asked of to transcend into a new way of being. It can feel like we quickly shift through the soul cycle and our transcendence becomes more evident. Advanced soul work makes self-actualisation possible. It might take many years to master, but our continuous dedication to evolve our soul leads eventually towards our natural state. It is a rite given to all those who seek. We are being called to become closer and back to a state of wholeness. I invite you to let your mind and heart open to the Truth, let your Ego subside and invite the presence of something greater to become *known* to you. Follow the natural rhythm of where you feel guided to go next, it will always lead you to where you need to be.

WHERE IS SPIRIT AND YOUR SOUL GUIDING YOU?

PART VI
SELF-ACTUALISATION

Master Thy Self

Knowing others is wisdom.
Knowing the Self is enlightenment.
Mastering others requires force;
Mastering the Self needs strength.

He who knows he has enough is rich.
Perseverance is a sign of will power.
He who stays where he is endures.
To die but not to perish is to be eternally present.

—TAO TE CHING

LESSONS FOR YOUR SOUL

Once you complete a lesson there's a transcendental learning that takes place. Your Soul Blueprint has specifically been designed to give you exactly what you need to learn. Most likely you are not going to experience all life lessons or themes possible in this life. You've accumulated so much wisdom from many lifetimes experiencing different lessons. There are advanced souls, though. Some advanced souls—those who have mastered specific lessons—comeback to accelerate their learning to act as a guide in the afterlife. As a part of the process, they need to report back all of their learnings to their Council of 12 so they can use this collective information to assist shifting human consciousness to a higher state of awareness. Unless we have experienced some form of understanding from a human perspective what it's like to go through this lesson, we may find it harder to help others. Sometimes you care so much for a soul, or your soul family that you come down into this incarnation to accelerate their learning. This may include you undergoing unpleasant experiences. In some cases, you're helping them to shift their karma. It's only through coming into soul heart and wisdom, life experience and a level of understanding, can you transcend forms of lower thought vibrations that keep you or others stuck in the karmic cycle. There is a presence about those who have a big purpose and know how to become an expression of their soul. They act and think differently but make a purposeful difference just by being them. These are the advanced souls who just have an innate knowing that they are here to make a difference. Whether it's for one life, including themselves, or many. I want to say, if this resonates with you, you know deep in your heart that you can't ignore the challenges or lessons that get sent your way. You are here to step up in your full light. To live a life of soul by following your intuition, solidifying your faith in the Universe and showing others how to as well. You can feel the presence of spirit working with you, ensuring that you are always aligned with your purpose because your sacred mission is too precious to fail. Your specific soul lessons will also help others who are going through the same thing and it's why you might attract the same people but it doesn't matter because deep down, whether you're conscious of it or not, you are ready to fulfil your sacred mission. It's what you've been called here to do. Now, you are ready to access the information you need in order to fulfil your mission.

> ### SOUL MASTERY LESSON
> Ask your Council of 12 to help you to access your Akashic records for you and to filter it through your consciousness what information and insight is right for you to access in this moment. These insights can come through dreams, feelings, intuition, synchronicities, or through others who act unconsciously as a vessel for your healing. Don't push for answers because you are ultimately the driver of your life. You will receive what you need to know in this moment. I found that when I pushed for an answer, I didn't get anything. I had to look first at what I needed to work on. Trust that you will receive what you need.

MASTER THYSELF

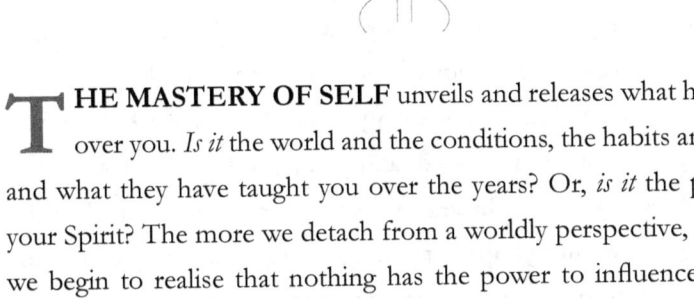

THE MASTERY OF SELF unveils and releases what has power over you. *Is it* the world and the conditions, the habits and beliefs and what they have taught you over the years? Or, *is it* the power of your Spirit? The more we detach from a worldly perspective, the more we begin to realise that nothing has the power to influence us, only what we allow. You can have either the power of Spirit flow through in your life, or the power of a limited humankind. Of course, there are certain limitations we have to abide by including laws, commitments, finances and bills that is how we function as a society. When we look at the bigger picture, we begin to expand our awareness in how much we can control.

When you don't feel that you're in control of life, reflect upon these questions: Who is in control? Where is the power? Have you become of the world or of your Spirit? When you are of the world, our feedback through emotional, mental and physical mechanisms tend to be that of an uninspiring state. From the world of Spirit, the world is not happening 'to you' as you aren't controlled by drama storms, mental or emotional manipulation to allow you to feel stuck in this world. Nothing has the power of you unless you give it permission to do so. When you release all of what is happening to you to Spirit, life unfolds for you. Lower mental thoughts and strong negative emotional charges are what can cause you to fall into the trap of getting stuck into the power of human will rather than the spiritual will. If we believe that human will is stronger than our spiritual will, that is what will transpire in our life. Remember, what you focus on expands. Come back into your centre—stillness—generate energy from your solar and heart centre. It's where you can generate the power of Spirit.

The key to staying in your power is to keep your heart open. This is how you keep your energy flowing and strengthening. Energy flows effortlessly when we keep our energy open. For example, have you ever received a call from a friend, and you leave the phone call energized after feeling flat? Or have you ever got a rush of energy because something that excites you is happening? This is our heart expanding and opening. Our mental and emotional processes influence the ability for energy to flow in your body. This is why it is so important to work on your mental and emotional state. It is why when you take moments out—get a healing, relax, exercise, do something out of routine—they are all shifting your internal state. I'm not talking about the energy you receive from food; this is the sustenance from life. As you open your heart more, you become less attached to negative thoughts, emotions or influences, you become open to the energy that exists all around you.

Waking up energized every day is not a figment of the imagination. It is a reality. It is in our biology. As we open our heart to love more, we begin to expand our awareness to love more of what is around us, the energy flows and allows us to seamlessly step into our soul power. As we approach each day, make a conscious choice to keep your heart open. Our instinctual nature is to protect our mind, body, emotions and Spirit. When we are exposed to the possibility of being hurt, we can shut down and close our heart flow. We try to conserve our energy. However, we have to make a conscious intention to keep our heart open. When we close our heart, we close our flow. This lowers our vibration and stops our ability to shift the situation to a higher state of consciousness.

Have you ever been in an argument where you felt attacked, then you attacked back and afterwards you felt emotionally drained? Being a heart warrior does not mean that you become passive, you can stick up for yourself but don't let it cost you your peace. The dimensions of the heart contain many elements. You can show love by speaking the truth with compassion and assertiveness at the same time, this is staying in your power. If you act out in spite, this is not a dimension of the heart. Your heart is a powerful organ and energy centre and as we begin to open up more, we realise how much we are actually connected to the Universal heart and we are acting out from this space.

You are meant to go through life, unpeeling layer by layer. Understanding yourself is the biggest gift you give to humanity. We are all made up of the same stuff. There are many things that we can't see that connects us all. This is not connecting you with an identity. This is the deepest part of your core that understands who you *truly* are. We are all the same, yet our personality helps to express an aspect of the Divine. If I told you who you are, you wouldn't be that. If you label it, that's not who you are. We only label things in this world, because we try to make meaning of it. Trying to understand who you are is something that you can't put into words or have a label for.

In this transcendental period there is nothing other than authenticity that shines through inside and out. It's all you know that you can be. Authenticity is another form of just knowing thyself through and through. When you know yourself, each action step that you take is a step towards self-actualisation because you know exactly what makes you thrive and feel that flow. You don't mind making those hard decisions because you know what's best for you as your thoughts are reflecting your Higher Self.

KNOWING WHO YOU ARE IS YOUR SUPER-POWER IN LIFE. BEING ANYTHING OTHER THAN YOURSELF IS YOUR KRYPTONITE IN FULFILLING YOUR PURPOSE.

LIGHT WAY

We all have a choice to walk in the way of the light. It's safe to feel light around you. Choose to experience more lightness. Being stuck in emotions means that you haven't yet had the opportunity to transcend yourself into lightness. The path of lightness is a transcendental state of awareness. When you reflect back onto your journey from the start, life unfolded like the matrix. You couldn't understand what was happening or why people were acting the way that they do. In this state of awareness—Lightness—the perspective of the soul comes through. It's as if you can see everything and everyone operating in a certain way and you have a contentedness in your heart that things are working out perfectly. People's reactions don't affect you because you understand that they are only operating from their level of awareness. It's as if their negativity bounces right off you. When something is happening around you, it's as if you can say to yourself, *Stuff it, that's not my karma, nor something that I wish to align to*. You don't have to be stuck in the process, just be willing to transcend all that no longer serves you. We are learning to walk more in Lightness. The lighter we become, the more we invite our divine aspect to flow through. By being lighter we pave the way for others to experience the benefits of being of the Light. It is the glimmer of hope for humanity. Being Light becomes a magnetic force in attracting what we truly desire and what gives us real fulfilment in this life.

> ### SOUL MASTERY INQUIRY
> * How are you living lighter?
> * What choices can you make now that will assist you in feeling lighter?

DIVINE ASPECTS

"What you think, you become.
What you feel, you attract.
What you imagine, you create."
— BUDDHA

We all have the potential to live in a way that's an expression of the Divine. It would be limited if we felt that we are separate from Source. In this lifetime, we all have the potentiality to express certain or all potential aspects. It's not impossible. It's not just a blessing given to certain people like saints or certain famous activists. We all have this within us and the more we choose to transform any limiting thoughts, feelings or actions, we become closer to becoming an expression of our True Self. Those who we admire, may have amplified traits so we understand how we can exhibit the same type of qualities, balanced and for the best of all. I ask you to keep an open mind that anything is possible. Transcendental experiences are experienced by those who believe in the power of possibilities. The Divine itself is something that no words can express. We often don't see how alike we are to the Divine. We feel that there's a sort of separateness far from who we are, but let me tell you a little secret, we are actually all interwoven and interconnected to the Divine more than we can think. All you need to do is be open and be willing to this and it is truly possible. All that you go through has been for a reason. If you can choose to challenge the problems that come your way and see their blessings, you invite the opportunity for living more spirited moments. You are Becoming. It's time to see your divinity.

DIVINE CONNECTION

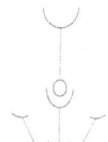
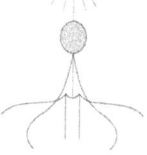

In fleeting moments, we remember and feel that we are all one with the Divine. Other times, as we navigate through this complex world, we feel detached from our true nature. In every moment, we are connected with everything that exists in this Universe. We are all made up of matter. We all matter.

At times, we are clouded by our thoughts and can't feel that energy flow through our being. Connection is what rules everything. Connection is what makes a difference and impacts us and others. When our awakening process began, it helped to open our world to the connection to something mystical that you could not even comprehend. As the journey progresses, we let go of anything that makes us feel disconnected. Any process signifies a time for us to truly understand our connection. Deep down we have always known what it feels like to be connected to unconditional love. Those who feel that separation or loneliness deeply is because they understand from a deeper level what it's like to be fully loved and supported. In the Spirit world, there is only love and peace. Any time we feel lonely, we have to navigate ways in which we can feel that reconnection. Even though, there is never truly a disconnect. It's only a sign that a part of our ego has crept through and we've overcomplicated our thoughts or there is a subconscious thought that is needing to be pulled out like a weed in a garden of magic. There will always be someone or Spirit there for you. If we can soldier on and transcend our thoughts on feeling lonely, we give ourselves a chance for our whole being to feel connected. You can't change circumstances, but you can change how much energy you'd like to flow through you and how much love you can receive.

We choose to either make our connection strong or weak. It's like a Wi-Fi signal, the more we remove ourselves from our spiritual practices or operating choices out of fear, we weaken our ability to understand or hear our intuitive guidance. The more we choose actions out of love, the more we are operating from the Divine. It's so important to choose to create stronger connections in your life. This is to the Divine, yourself, others and the world. As our connections strengthen, we begin to understand our potential as a powerful human soul. Like a team, we are all vibrating atoms, having different functions in the world, living out our purpose perfectly.

The stronger we have of our connection to our sense of Self and the Divine, the more we unfold the connection we have with others. Our soul family are the people we hold dearly in our life, and the people who challenge us love us too. Understanding both the Divine and Self, allows you to know others and see beyond just their physical body. You can see through to their soul light. This is the highest perception we can attain, looking through the eyes of the soul. An understanding of the heart, rather than the understanding of the matter you perceive in front of you. Others are acting as the True Self, as you are. We are all expressions of the Divine, no matter how connected or not you perceive the other to be. The most spiritual act we can take is being ourselves. Whatever that looks like in that perceived moment. We are all co-creating with the cosmos, strengthening our connection back to our true home. A continuous practice of meditation is one of the strongest gateways to strengthen your connection.

> ### SOUL MASTERY LESSON
> * Do what you can to strengthen your connection. Meditate to accelerate!
> * When you're feeling off participate in practices that help you stay connected.
> * Our self-actualised Self strengthens our connections to Self and others.

DIVINE MIND

Transcendental thoughts will help you to access the divine mind. You have to be willing to not attach yourself to lower thought forms. It can be really tricky from a human perspective because it can be so much easier to fall into the trap of judgement, hate, anger, resentment or fear. Our judgments are what help us to navigate through this world. It is our survival mechanism. However, how can we access that ability to think from a higher perspective? The perspective of the divine mind. We have to do the work to access these particular thought forms. You have to be willing to see things from other perspectives. This is what makes us a better human.

Our mind is one of the most human parts of us. Its filtering system is what helps us to connect to others and filter through the world. Like a hierophant or priestess, we become a messenger of the Divine to shift the collective consciousness. We learn to speak the language of the heart, rather than the limited mind because our thoughts become one with the ever-present stream of universal consciousness. You know you have this aspect within when you easily see that each action you or someone else makes has a purpose. It's almost as though you have an innate ability to see beyond their actions and you can see how everything is falling perfectly into place.

How can we tell the difference between our ego or divine mind? The ego operates from complexity. Have you ever noticed that when you have a perceived problem you think about all the things that are going wrong or could go wrong? You might replay the situation over and over in your mind. However, the divine mind can only see the blessings, the real universal truth in each and every moment. It's easy to get caught up in the drama that humanity has stirred, but it can be just as easy to show up each day thinking from a higher perspective. As you continue to transcend your thoughts to higher thoughts, seeing things from a higher perspective, you'll begin to feel that endless stream of consciousness run through you.

Your mind is a transmitter. Whatever you focus on expands. Your mind is a critical component because it becomes an important aspect to where you will channel your energy. As you continue to open your mind, the Universe is able to filter through more intuitive insights into your being. If you're stuck in lower thought forms, it brings about ambiguity and clouds your judgements. It's much stickier in your auric layer. You'll create experiences that are matching this. Attune your thoughts to the Divine and you'll begin to become a co-creator with the Universe.

In an inspired state of consciousness, you are not worried about who enters your field. It's actually your mind that helps stabilize your mental, emotional and physical layer. We can focus so much on trying to work through processes that we neglect actually strengthening our mind. I had done so many healings, working through progress, that I never realised until a few years later that making my mind stronger, played a profound part in helping me to move forward in my life.

The soul seeks expansion. You might not be in the state of pure bliss all the time, but you have the ability and power to be powerfully minded in more moments of your life. The greatest way to strengthen your mind is to align your thoughts with powerful affirmations. 'I AM' statements affirmed in the positive, then see and feel these affirmations in your physiology. Your mind plays a big part in channelling that high state of consciousness and helping to bring an inspired physiology in. This is only through just a thought. How miraculous is that!

Many people make the mistake to just clean up their energy through healings or just focus on one thing to work on: physical, emotional or energetically. You need more than just one ingredient to make a cake and this is just like when we are creating a fulfilling life. We need to work on all aspects of our being. One is not more important than the other to work on. It's critical to work on all aspects so that we are balanced and feeling more complete. The mind is misunderstood. When we truly learn to transcend our thoughts, we are able to see how our mind is like that of the Divine. Not separate.

Our mind controls our attitudes, beliefs and actions. If we are attuned to the divine mind, then we will only act out of that which is for the highest good of all. In a relaxed state, we are able to access the executive function part of our brain which assists us in tuning into our intuition and allowing better focus and clarity to any solution that we need to have in our life. When we are in a heightened state, we attune back to our primitive nature, which makes us feel that the world is attacking us on a physical, emotional and mental layer. The primitive part of our brain is what distorts our perceptions on the world. Our personality, which is made up of what we believe of ourselves, when aligned to your highest calling, will act out accordingly to the divine plan. Our personality marries our gifts perfectly. Whatever our nature is that is comfortable for you, whether you use humour or have a serious nature, is the way you're meant to navigate through this world. It's your personality that will connect others to you. A balanced personality never delves into that state of the ego. The ego isn't a dirty word. I describe the ego as an over or under stimulated personality that is acting out of fear. Let's take the view of your personality as your actions that reflect your soul gifts that will ultimately help assist you with your soul's calling. Without it, we can't do the one thing that's so critical for humanity, and that's to connect. Our mind is the most human part of us, without our personality, others can't connect with you.

I know that I'm a massive overthinker. I know that when I'm in an overthinking stage, I've kind of let my spirited Self go. The more we overthink things, the more we know that we are acting out the state of the ego and it's time to redirect our thoughts to Spirit. Your mind is a funnel for the Universe. All you need to do is point and direct, and then 'thy will be done.'

SOUL MASTERY LESSON

* Your mind is a powerful component that directs energy where it needs to go.
* Your personality compliments your soul gifts and your divine purpose.
* Guidance is easily received when you're attuned to higher frequency thought forms.
* Set intentions to align to a higher perspective, which is the wisdom of the soul.

DIVINE HEART

Do you ever feel you think and act differently to others? This is most likely because you operate from your heart, rather than your mind. When your awakening comes about, it shatters the ego and helps provide the gateway to your heart. I know that in this lifetime, I have always felt a little bit different to others. Even when people have not been the kindest, I've always still had the ability to see beyond their actions and see them for the treasure that they are. Sometimes it's annoying because I just want to get angry at another person for treating me a certain way but there's something within my heart that stops me from engaging in any form of negative emotions towards another person for too long. I'm sure some of you can really relate to this. The heart is designed to discern the Truth from your soul. This is why what we feel can see beyond someone's actions. You are able to see the wisdom on what's truly happening for yourself or another in that moment. That Truth is what stops you from engaging in any form of negativity towards another because you just can't.

The mind, the ego, would argue that this is not a blessing because it is easier to hate someone than love them. You can't teach heart intelligence. You're just a good human being in a world that you feel doesn't always operate from this space. For many Lightworkers, the heart is their greatest strength. It's what has been birthed strongly for many so that we can create constructive change in this world. It is one of the most powerful places to live from. If you operate mostly from this space, then it's important for you to stay as much heart centred as possible. It's a gift to see through the eyes of the heart. Heart intelligence is not understood from an intellectual level. You might be the type that can pick up people's feelings straight away or before they even know what's stirring within them and you can understand the way people operate because you see the reasons behind a behaviour, rather than just seeing them from the actions that they make.

At the start of my awakening process, I had a friend who didn't understand how I could be so happy and loving all the time. The more I spent time with this friend, her thoughts became mine and I started to judge myself for being heart centred. I was conned into thinking that it was the wrong place to be because how could I be so naïve about the world? It led me to so much judgement and eventually tears. I felt more disconnected because I saw the world through a victim mentality rather than a higher perspective. It took about three years to undo the beliefs that became my conditioning. Although she meant well, we were polar opposites as she had her heart closed to the world, and my heart was very open. I didn't enjoy where I was. When we are not aligned with our heart space then the world becomes not enough. The heart always feels content and peace with the world. We all act as a catalyst for each other's change. I needed to learn the power of the heart. The experience only made me more determined to stay in my heart space and not compromise myself for anyone. My heart is my spark. This is for so many of you too. Never compromise your heart that shines, because others can't understand it.

The heart is the most powerful gateway for constructive change. The heart emits its own frequency, and this is even backed up by science. You will feel more open, around loving people, and feel more shut off around those who might find it hard to connect. It's your job to stay as open as possible in each and every moment. Even if there's a possibility for your heart to close in a challenging situation or around people who cause conflict, by keeping your heart open, you change not only karmic patterns, but you create an opportunity for healing and love to take place. If you come up to a situation where you feel your heart energy is closing up, ask for assistance in keeping it open and finding peace in that situation.

SOUL MASTERY AFFIRMATION

I can easily keep my heart energy open and find peace, love and joy in each and every moment. When my heart is open, I offer the opportunity to open other hearts so that they can operate from the heart space. Please assist me to keep an open heart with _____ so that the divine can be present for both _____ and myself.

Wishing blessings for others, brings blessings for you. Love, gratitude and appreciation is the space that the heart will always operate from.

SOUL MASTERY INQUIRY

* What would a divine heart look like for you in your life?
* How are you already showing this or have shown this in your life?
* How can you incorporate more of the heart space in other areas of your life?

> * Who needs to be shown more love, even if you find it challenging?

As you crack open your heart more, you help to crack open the heart of others. Stay raw, vulnerable and open. The heart helps to soften others to get into their heart space. There's a misconception that being softer is weak. There is more strength and courage in operating from you heart, because it is easier to hide away. As you know yourself more, you know that any reaction caused by another cannot affect you because you know your true identity and their empty words which is trying to cause a reaction can't affect you. Words are only as powerful as what you make them. When I've engaged with people who are unwilling to listen, I try not to engage in their powerplay, I breathe, and soften. You slowly can make small adjustments in this space. As a teacher, I have even had challenging kids. In the times where I worked as a substitute teacher, I had kids trying to test the limits. When I stayed calm and operated from the heart, they could see that I actually cared and didn't bother testing the limits or were quite mellow. If I reacted in a forceful way, which a lot of teachers do, this just escalates the situation and makes things worse. We want to ensure that with every conscious decision we make, we are making situations and circumstances better.

THE HEART HAS
THE POWER TO
TRANSFORM
LIVES.
KEEP YOUR
HEART OPEN.
HEART
INTELLIGENCE
IS A GIFT.

DIVINE CREATOR

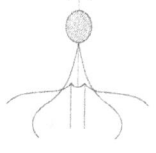

"You'll see it, when you believe it."
– WAYNE DYER

There is magic within our being when we are be-ing. As our hearts and thoughts are aligned to our highest calling and into the now. We know our potential as a creator. In each and every moment we are a powerful creator. We never realise how much power we have over our lives until we take some time out to bring our awareness to see how every choice that we make eventuates. Every decision we have ever made in our life, has caused us to be where we are right now. It's funny to think we've created everything in our life right now. Even when certain experiences have occurred, we still have been in control of our thoughts, feelings, actions and reactions.

As we fine tune to the frequency of the Universe, our mind and the collective becomes one. In this state, we are able to play with the Universe things that we wish to manifest in our life. Some people don't realise that we can't put just any thought out to the Universe and expect it to come straight away without any sort of purposeful action. In order to create the life we wish we have to show up as much as the Universe does each day. Anything that you know is possible can come true for you. When you have the thoughts of a creator you know that what you desire comes from the wishes of a pure heart, rather than what we think should be our hearts desires. A lot of people may crave to be financially abundant and financial security is so important, but would you like to gain this by doing something that doesn't make you feel good on the inside? Financial abundance can be possible in conjunction with your soul gifts. You have to believe that it's possible and you're worthy to receive what you desire.

Coming to the realisation of the power that exists within you as a powerful creator, allows you the freedom to create any experience you wish to desire. To step into your capacity of a conscious creator, you have to fully love and accept the power within you. A Divine Creator is benevolent, and all creative possibilities are those which expand your soul as well as assist humanity. You have the capacity to create powerful change in this collective consciousness. When you discover your magic, you become a co-creator with the Universe. Maybe you know someone who just clicks their fingers and it seems that everything is done under their command. There was a time when I was in Hawaii that my friend wanted chocolate cake. It was a very random request. Her intentions were specific and clear. She felt and thought about it. We decided to eat out that night. We met for dinner and you wouldn't believe it, we got complimentary chocolate cake from the waiter who was not present at our discussion. You can't even make this stuff up. Clear intention, thoughts, feelings and actions help to create manifestations into reality. We weren't expecting to receive a cake, we surrendered that expectation over. The best manifestations come when we release our expectations. This experience showed that the Universe always delivers something delicious when we are in the right energy. You might be thinking, this was only just a chocolate cake but imagine what's possible when we start to think bigger!

My friend, Ally, she is a magical creator. It's as if she knows innately the laws of the Universe work for her. When she needs money, it magically appears. When she needs a job, there's an offering straight away. She declares it and it's almost as if she becomes a magnet to whatever she puts out there. It's not that she has magical abilities that others don't have. It's because she's learnt to trust, have faith and utilise the powerful manifestation powers that the Universe presents itself.

Have a play with the Universe. I remember when I was wanted to meet a partner, I was feeling super emotional and hardly went out. I didn't know how it was going to be even possible for me to make that a reality. So, I declared to the Universe: How am I meant to meet anyone if I'm going through my emotional processes? It's as if the Universe laughed and said, 'We'll show you!' For two months, every Tuesday, I would meet some random who gave me their number. Whether it was walking down the street to get a coffee or even just being in my car. Somehow, I had created opportunities with the Universe to receive what I had put out there.

> **If something is meant to be for your path, the path will be created for you.**

Your soul knows that it is a miracle worker. You can't deny what's a part of you. Adopt a miracle mentality. Expect miracles and allow the Universe to surprise you. Faith is prevalent when it comes to becoming a miracle creator. All creative phases go through a process. The beauty of our human existence is that we can see the birth of creation slowed down. As a soul we can instantly manifest anything and that's where some of our angst can bubble up when we understand on a deep level our creator potential. Surrender into the process and have faith that all is working in your favour. You have to believe in miracles for miracles to work for you.

SOUL MASTERY AFFIRMATION

I am a miracle worker. My possibilities are unlimited. Please align my thoughts and actions with the Divine, so we can co-create a magnificent reality together aligned with my highest calling.

When I needed to get out of my workplace a few years ago, I prayed and meditated every night. There was a sense of peace in my heart knowing that somehow a job will miraculously present itself. I came to this workplace in desperation to get out of my other job. I needed an out. I was done. I didn't think about what I wanted my next workplace to be like. I just needed to leave, and I knew I wanted a wellbeing job. Well, there was a wellbeing job and I got it. That year was extremely hard. I knew I wanted out again, which was slightly annoying, but I knew that the next space that I needed to go to, I needed to put out to the Universe what I wanted to experience. Therefore, instead of just focusing on the type of job I wanted I thought about exactly what I wanted to experience and feel. I also surrendered the need for a label or title. I asked the Universe to place me where I could firstly be of service and secondly, to give me that which would give me the greatest fulfillment. This is what I meditated on. I spent one afternoon creating a mandala where I began to channel what I wanted to feel and experience in my next workplace. I wasn't panicking about where and when I'd find a job. For some reason, I had a feeling that a job would just appear. Two weeks later, I found a school where a job had opened up and was offered an amazing opportunity. It was everything that I had intended for in a job. A new role was created, close to home. This was perfect for me. I believe that the Universe works with us when we learn how to work with each other. Faith, trust and surrendering is a big part of the creation process. I gave time for the seed to be planted so that the Universe could help with the blooming stage. The creation process is cyclic in nature. Trust the process, and you can flourish. You water your seed by allowing it time to bloom. This is the secret to your manifesting power.

SOUL MASTERY INQUIRY

* What is ready to be created into this world?
* What is something that has come magically and made you believe in miracles?
* What is one thing that you can do to activate your ability to manifest miracles? Give yourself time to process and find the answer, and then write it in your journal. Miracles can present through the illogical.
* What am I wanting to manifest right now and how can I begin to think bigger?
* Grab your journal. Think about something you wish to manifest right now. Meditate on this. Divide your page in half. On one side write down what you need to do, on the other side write what the Universe needs to do.
* Visualise something you wish to manifest in your life right now. You can start with something small. Write down these intentions. Feel them. See them in your mind's eye. What are the

actions that you need to make in order for it to manifest for you? What will the Universe do for you? Be specific with your intentions and surrender into it. You are now becoming a co-creator with the Universe.

SOUL MASTERY AFFIRMATION

I am fully activating my creative potential.

DIVINE PURPOSE

Throughout our life we might not realise that we have always been drip fed slowly our purpose, even in our most unawakened state. There is a deep sense that we have known all along what we are meant to do or who we are meant to become. Our soul knows, and it unfolds to your consciousness more and more as you live your journey. We are constantly given signs or inklings, where we need to be next. Make it clear, your purpose is not a destination but an accumulation of purposeful moments.

Our divine purpose is measured by two principles stated by the Greeks. Chronos and Kairos. Chronos refers to the ordered time that we live by on Earth, it is measured. The other Kairos, this is qualitative, which is the right time at the right moment and the purposeful events that are occurring in the present moment. These two principles work together to create the perfect moment for you. As you are truly aligned with your being, we live by Kairos time. Our destined moments become more apparent. Kairos is perfectly constructed. There is a trust that you can't put parameters into what is already perfectly constructed and it's in the non-constraints that brings about divine perfection and illuminates your being.

Be the Light you were born to be. In this phase of your life, no-one can ever take away from you what you truly are. If you're going to choose to be the Light, be the shiniest version of yourself. You become a presence that's felt for miles. It's naturally going to gravitate people towards you and experiences that reflect your essence. Remember a time when you were shining and flowing as one with the Universe, always tap back into this moment if you're wanting to experience your best Self when you're feeling off. It's not the time to believe others when they judge you for being true to you. In your true form, you are transforming lives unintentionally. A light heart, mind and energy helps life, even when it's challenging, to feel effortless. Let's light up the world like a Christmas tree bringing so much love, blessings and support to ourselves and anyone that needs it. A light frequency vibrates fast. Therefore, anything that is dense will receive a shake-up. It will generate movement to help lift others to access the dimension of their heart space which has the ability to transform and transmute all lower thought, emotional and physical forms.

Each and every moment is constantly fine tuning us to our highest potentiality. Our divine purpose is to help bring the light, our special gifts, and illuminate it to the world. Our gifts are made up of lightness because it helps to bring magic in others' lives and when we are fully connected, we are feeling light, as if we are floating in the air. Our soul gifts are unique depending on what we are wanting to do in this lifetime which is all consistent with our growth and evolutionary process. Therefore, it is important to not compare yourself to others and to fully love and embrace who you are. All your talents and perceived flaws. When you learn to truly love and accept yourself and see the beauty of you, you can fully embrace what you're here to do and how you can do it. As your gifts become fully actualised, so will your life purpose.

Clarity always brings about purposeful actions.

Some people believe that their life purpose is a destination. Your life purpose is made up of many assignments to complete. Your assignments become focused on not only helping yourself but in helping others. It evolves and transcends. Assignments come in the form of helping to transform your lessons and learn to help others with theirs. It's as if the moment we put our hand up and say, *I'm ready to fulfil my life purpose*, that at a rapid rate we are sent all these assignments that lead us to fulfil our soul wishes. A soul wish is to make a real difference to this world through service. This might not serve our ego, but this is what becomes true fulfilment on a soul level. We are meant to have a life that's fulfilling and the more that we discover who we are, inside and out, the more we are able to make choices which are soulful and aligned to who we are. As self-actualisation becomes realistic, more synchronistic moments occur because we are flowing with our spirit, rather than the constraints of the mind. There's a certain trust and faith that everything is occurring how it's meant to.

Everything that occurs in your life, acts as more of an opportunity to be more of what you are, Light. Life presents itself, guiding you in each and every moment to be more of who you are. Life is happening to you in a way that will always support you to being aligned to your True Self. If you've come into this lifetime willing to be fully expressed as your soul, life will only illuminate that which is your true nature. Life becomes a knowing that it is purposeful. Each and every moment exists for immense potentiality. It's going to pull you away from the darkness in order for you to fully step into your soul light. Circumstances, people or particular habits may completely have to go in your life, and even though it might break your heart, the universe is operating for your highest good. From a higher perspective, we understand that everything is in order and our guides are working with us to ensure that the path that's required for soul fulfillment, will be manifested. Attachments form a golden opportunity for learning. From a limited perspective, we cling to our attachments and stay stuck because we judge the circumstances that are occurring to us. Whereas if you are transcending each and every experience, you are allowing more light to come through and this is leading you to a life of living each day, every moment, in your ultimate purpose.

When I've acted from my gut feelings and followed intuitive insights, I've found that my purpose has been shown to me. I've learnt never to go with anything that hasn't allowed my heart to expand. This is how I base most of my decisions. Whatever presents itself I ask, does this make my heart feel expansive? If it feels tight, I know it's a no. If it feels warm and open, I know it's a yes. I commit to my heart choices because I know that I'm being guided. Faith and trust in our intuition can take time but we have to be clear that the universe *will* act always for our highest good. Being a Lightworker, we can be so supportive and loyal to others, rather than ourselves. As we have gone through our spiritual journey, we begin to realise more of the blessings and importance it is to be loyal to yourself. In full alignment, it's as if expectations for certain things to run a certain way disappear and your knowingness for things to manifest shows up magically because you are tapped into the divine magical flow of your being.

My friend, Conor, is a perfect example on how when you only follow a spark of an idea, how it just unfolds for you. Conor is passionate about health and always has been. When he was in Byron, his soul home, he was at a spa just relaxing where he got an idea to get an infrared sauna. He had never had an infrared sauna session before but felt it was right for him to purchase one. He knew a place where he could possibly rent a space in. So, he thought he would take a punt on it. The effortless flow that took place next could not be expected. As soon as he started, his business boomed. It became so financial abundant that he had no choice but to expand. It gave him financial freedom and it allowed him to also study his passion, naturopathy and live in Bali. His life path, which might've seemed illogical, opened up an expansion to bigger and greater things. It opened the gateway for him to open up a wellness centre that incorporated all of his passions into one and to give back to the world. If you ask him what he wants to do, his answer is to give back to the world and offer freely the potential healing for all to experience. His alignment came through being in a space that aligns with his soul, creating time to be still and following an idea that might some out of the blue, but felt that it was right. It led him to a channel of pure abundance, and everything fell into place effortless. It might've been an unconventional channel for financial abundance, but it was the best way to support his divine purpose. Your true divine purpose will always help others in some shape or form. He didn't have to do anything but show up.

Another time when I was with Conor, we decided to go to the beach and just make some wishes with the ocean. With the flow of the ocean we decided that as the water went away from the shore, we intentionally allowed the waves to let go of everything that was holding us back from moving forward. When the water came in, we imagined that we were receiving the blessings of the Universal flow. As we sat and meditated, we both began to receive clear guidance about our next steps. I had almost finished this book and already had different book concepts I was working on. But what I received was an image of a book title, the flow of what I needed to work on next. It was quite magical. I wasn't expecting to receive any guidance, but I had created a state where I could easily connect better. It was the only flash of inspiration that I received but it all started with just a thought. I allowed space for that thought by intentionally letting go. I felt filled with inspiration and couldn't wait to get started. Like this book, it just started with a thought and I watched it unfold. All I had was a book title and what it was a guide for. I grabbed my notebook, which I always carry with me, and just started to brainstorm some ideas. I was so surprised how the information became effortless. I have come to this point in my journey now to know that when it feels effortless and my heart expands that's my next step. That's all it has to start with. It's like the Universe places that spark, to activate that seed that has been dormant in your being for so long, because the world is ready for it now. Not a year ago, but now and when you feel that internal push, you know that you need to respond with commitment and honour.

Your destiny will always show up when the timing is right. If you're working on a project, know that when the world is ready, it will truly come to the Light. Some ideas may be present for you now, but it might not be ready to manifest until ten years later and this is okay. If we rely heavily on how we expect life to be, we are only limiting ourselves for finite possibilities. If we push for those finite possibilities, you risk the ability to receive less blessings and flow in your life. If you feel that something isn't going anywhere, maybe it's not the time for it. When you continue to push and you are met with resistance, then that may be the sign that you need to take a step back and surrender. To receive more flow, there are times when you'll need to create the circumstances to be in a more receptive state. This is attained through choosing to engage in flow activities such as meditation, yoga or anything that brings you back into centre. Being pushy is pushing away the energy of grace. Yet, if you feel the need to move with momentum, flow with that. If what you want isn't coming into fruition, you can ask the Universe to help manifest it at the right time to allow you to focus on what needs to be focused on next. It might even be that you change jobs to something unexpected because you need to make a connection, it brings you into a realisation on where you need to be, or it could be the best possible way to fund your dream. Ask that whatever needs to be focused on is what will become present in your awareness.

At times, when I've had the attitude of that I'll go and do something even if I fail, I've always noticed much more synchronistic moments than if I stayed back and did nothing. We can't always just wait for the Universe to do all the work. We have to meet the universe half-way. It takes courage to follow your life plan. It can feel unnatural because we've learnt from such a young age to follow the logistics and constraints of the mind, we have to adapt to a new way of being. The path of the soul is one of courage and unshakable faith. When you know yourself, the decisions you make become clearer and you have no regret because you know that whatever the outcome is, is what is exactly needed for you. You have the clarity that you need to make actions that cause an impact. Being self-assured in who you are, becomes the best alignment for you to manifest your divine purpose. This is why your alignment is so pivotal. It shapes who you are. As you discover more about yourself, the easier your life decisions become. You will naturally change over time as you are always a masterpiece at work. Whatever purposeful action you choose to make that is in pure alignment with all aspects of yourself, your gifts and talents will naturally shine in each and every moment. Thus, fulfillment is present in every moment. Wherever you show you, you understand that on a deep core level that it's the exact place you're meant to be, illuminating and sharing more of yourself—this is your divine purpose.

Have fun along the way. You'll notice that you become magnetic for what you need for your divine purpose. Take a light heart. This is how you can enjoy the journey. Our life is defined by perceptions and your ability to fulfil your destiny will be shaped on the perceptions that you have on life. In this high-vibe energy, you can make high vibrational decisions. Clarity on what you're worthy of and desire, plus being immersed into joy, will be the momentum you need to fulfil your divine destiny. Manifestation of your dreams occurs with more than just a thought. Dreams and desires only come true when they come from the pure alignment of your heart and anything that supports your dreams. If you have full peace in this present moment, knowing in your heart and soul that everything that is occurring to you is for your highest good, it will open more gateways for you to receive the blessings of the Universe. You are more of a miracle worker than you could ever imagine. It's time to activate that miracle worker mentality.

Your true purpose serves in some shape or form. Align to fame and you'll attract people in your life aligned to the materialistic world. The quality of people in your life will not feel as fulfilling because they are addicted to the manly world, which is the opposite to the flow of Spirit. Aligned to serving the world, you will attract financial abundance and possibly fame because you weren't asking for that. If you're truly a vessel of the Universe, this will automatically spread and express itself. The power of your potential is unlimited.

You'll receive the next steps for your soul growth when you're least expecting it. Your divine purpose is unfolding exactly how it's meant to be right now in this moment.

Prayer

Please assist me in my full alignment to my highest calling.

SOUL MASTERY LESSON

* Listen and follow your soul calling.
* It's in the small action steps we feel in our heart that makes the difference.
* Have fun along the way.
* Know that you're never off your path.
* You're always aligned to your soul purpose.
* Each present moment unfolds your true purpose in life.
* Consciously choose to live a life of Light.
* You are here to be a catalyst of change for the highest good of all.
* When you show up, your purpose does too.
* Be receptive to the grace of the Universe.
* You are here for a reason.

DIVINE PRESENCE

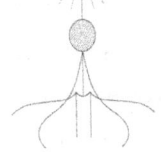

I AM THAT I AM.

You can't really put into words the endless stream of divine energy that is *you*. When you're truly in an inspired state, do you notice how you can just walk into a room and people can automatically feel you? It's as if your physical body becomes translucent and you are like the sun, lighting up the room. Your energy expands, and it feels you are touching every aspect of that room, yet still staying in your physical body. We can no longer show up being small. With this expanded awareness of our divine aspects, we are consciously choosing to take control of our lives. This new level of perception means that we start to take full ownership of what we create right in front of us.

> **We are all being called to step up, own our Light and live out our Presence.**

You are accountable for your conscious actions. You are taking ownership of every part of your life. Our transcendental soul knows that to operate from anything other than our divine aspects feels unnatural. As the Universe flows more through you, you begin to realise that we are more of a soul having a human experience than just a soul trapped in a human.

The power of the **I AM Presence** is that you don't need to be anything but THAT. To be specific, when you say, 'I Am THAT, I Am,' you are declaring and aligning all your thoughts and energy to your true and divine presence. In this state, you are proclaiming **I am my divine presence, my true Self.** This is a powerful statement. Imagine what you are able to create when you are in that expanding sense of Self and consciousness. You become your most spirited Self.

YOU ARE LIGHT, YOU ARE THAT HEART EXPANSION, YOU ARE EVERYTHING.

I AM THAT I AM.

SELF-ACTUALISATION SUMMARY

All things are made possible with Spirit and your soul. If you understood your potential, doubt would never come into play. The Divine is present within all of us and we are *becoming* an expression of its Will. If you can open your heart and mind enough for this consciousness to pierce through for you, the floodgates of blessings come pouring out for you. This blessing hasn't just been bestowed amongst the Saints or Ascended Masters who walked this Earth, they only showed the way that it's possible for you to achieve this and come back to your true state. The world has come to a point where it needs to remember. It's been stuck in its karmic patterns and ways for too long that has been having a negative impact not only on human beings but on the Earth too. Your becoming and self-actualising is really you remembering who you *truly* are and what your main mission has been here to do. It takes great mastery of the mind and integration of your soul presence to fully shine through. We are remembering and learning how to *be* a human *being* again.

The Divine is present through your actions and it has been our soul mission, whether conscious or unconscious, to live out its expression. We may be learning how to become one of these expressions throughout this lifetime or possibly master a few because we are becoming integrated into a presence that cannot be explained, only experienced. Mastery is made possible when you truly accept and understand that something beyond is orchestrating your experiences, yet you feel so aligned that it feels as if what your heart desires and what Spirit wants has become one. Your intentions are the same. Here you know deep down in your heart that you've begun to break out of all illusions or traps that have kept you in a state of stagnancy or suffering. You are in full alignment.

You are experiencing the Truth, Light and I AM Presence that is always with you. The Divine is made known through you and you can finally see what the ancients knew all along existed within you. Whether this phase lasts a lifetime or just a small moment because there might be other lessons that need to be made, learn to accept what has always been your birthright.

YOU HAVE BECOME AN EXPRESSION OF THE DIVINE.

A BLESSING

Light a candle.

Bow your head as a sign of respect for the benevolent beings that love you unconditionally and help you along your path to reach self-actualisation.

To the Universal Life Force that flows through you and each and every one of you.

May the presence of the Divine become integrated into your being and can be felt from all the senses and on all levels in your consciousness now.

The eyes of the Divine, *may you be blessed to see through the perspective of the Divine. May all illusions be lifted to allow the heart of unconditional love to enter through your eyes.*

The thoughts of the Divine, *may your insights, wisdom and thoughts reflect that of a Divine presence that is within you.*

The words of the Divine, *may your words be an expression of true Divine presence. An expression of unconditional love, support, healing, wisdom and true power.*

The heart of the Divine, *may you feel the ever presence of every single thing that exists on the planet as oneness. May each and every interaction be felt and known with the heart that all that exists are all expressions of something greater than ourselves. May we have the courage and compassion to exhibit forgiveness and love and see beyond the illusions that people are playing out. The heart's perspective that anything other than love and gratitude exist.*

The conscious actions of the Divine, *may your actions be the fullest expression of the Divine. May your actions inspire others to live on purpose and in service to humanity. May all your actions be in full alignment to your Higher Self living out your highest purpose.*

The presence of the Divine*, may the 'I AM' presence be actively activated and engaged fully online in your Soul Blueprint. May the awareness and flow of life exist simultaneously through you.*

I AM THAT, I AM.

Whatever 'that' is for you, it's true nature will become manifested for you. Your creator mode activated, fully aligned and online. May the presence of the Divine express itself through your vessel. Acting as a reminded and activator for others that the Divine is ever present in our life. Every atom is vibrating, connected in oneness.

May you be blessed to 'reawaken' and allow the power of the Divine to come through for you. May its presence live out in each and every moment of your day. All you need to do is ask and you will receive.

Thank you for allowing me to find the joy in life. Our divine Self is joy.

Thank you. Thank you. Thank you.

In love and gratitude. xx

Soak it all up. Those good vibes. Good things are coming your way because you're worthy to receive it. It's time to reignite that belief and knowing truth of your divine nature. There's no guilt or shame in divine love. It's time to release that guilt, shame, sadness, fear or pride you've had throughout your missing years. Breathe in deeply. Breathe out and let it all go.

SOUL MASTERY

Our journey as a soul is always to return back to Source energy. All paths lead to the expansion of our soul. We are all walking a journey differing from others. Our ability to transform our mind and body makes us powerful creators in our own right. Our humanness is meant to be experienced. Our body is like a wetsuit encasing our soul, protecting us from the dangers of the water—life—but it *all* comes equipped with what you need to get through life.

As our awareness expands, we become what we started from. When you were born, your needs were simplistic. All you craved for was love and that your basic needs were met. As you began to discover the world, the worldly conditions began to make things complicated. Words gave meaning to objects and you could label things. Our mind began to be aware of right and wrong and then the world became an intertangled web of mixed messages and difficulties. Your *initiation* and *awakening* began to bring you back into balance and back to real life. You are being given another chance at life and now you're at a stage in your life where you're ready to make empowered choices for your soul.

What causes a stir within your being to change, have the courage to do it. Follow the path of least resistance. We can sometimes be so afraid to change, that we blame the universe for our suffering when it truly is a part of our soul's calling to change. We need to change in order to break down lifetimes of habits and conditions that no longer serve us. The work you do makes a change to the ancestors before you and creates a ripple effect on the future of your offspring and family.

We can choose to be small or live a large fulfilling life. This is what the universe wishes for us, to experience a life of pure nourishment for the mind, body and soul. A nourished life is one where you can come to love and appreciate all that occurs and know that deep down everything is working out for you, even when it's hard to accept temporarily. Our ego grasps onto suffering, our soul embraces freedom. Although we may be challenged to change and can feel off-centre, the Lightworker knows that the best way to get back to feeling aligned is surrendering and having the courage to come back to your spirited Self. Your spirited Self is its most radiant and wise Self. From changing the old ways, you're able to shed your skin and emerge with new understandings, perceptions and experiences with such delight. You take that soul knowledge and take time to integrate a new way of being. Breathe and take that in.

The ego makes things as complicated as possible by filtering through your thoughts and actions. It relies on holding onto fear, jealousy and hate towards the world and yourself. But you know it is a trap because in this lifetime, you weren't here to be stuck in your ego and others constructs of the world, rather you are here to be an expression of the Divine. You were born to rise and fully utilise all of what you bring to this world. Your Higher Self knows that the flow of Spirit is one of ease, beauty and love.

As you continue to peel back the layers of the ego, all of a sudden comes the realisation that the beauty of life comes in simplicity. A veil lifts. You become lighter. Your thoughts become light, connected to Source and you know in your heart that it's not what you have—the material possessions—and you begin to appreciate that what you already have is *enough*. You are enough.

At the end of our cycle of life, we leave the world, back to dust, leaving with nothing, other than our Spirit. The Spirit that has always been ever present. If we recreate more moments of simplicity, we come to attain peace. It doesn't mean the world will stop operating at a chaotic state, it just means that you operate in a state of peace. Wouldn't you rather a life of peace? That's your natural state. Your whole entire being craves it. An itch or inkling to become busy is only that when we have begun to lose the connection to our true Source. If we flow with the frantic pace of life, then we choose to flow with the world other than flowing with Spirit. Sometimes we may need to receive a kick in the right direction because it shows us where we are aligned to. We are always connected with the Divine and choosing to flow with this strengthens a life of magic and miracles.

The Mastery of Self can take a lifetime. You might not even master one area, but it's not about becoming the best Zen master. It's about how can we come as an expression of the Divine in each and every moment. We might not always act from this space, but our *awakening* helps us to make better choices to shift and expand the world's consciousness. Every lesson we make becomes an understanding on how we can be both heaven and earth manifested into this moment. We become an embodiment of the 'I AM presence.' We are Spirit, living a human experience learning how to integrate both aspects to become Spirman, *Spirit* and

Hu*man* combined. We are being called to bring about our most spirited Self. The most authentic, aligned and best version of yourself in every moment. This is what will transform the world and solidify your life purpose. Even when life can be a chaotic mess, this too might mean you're exactly where you need to be because your soul is growing and there's a rainbow in whatever is presented to you. There may be times when you may feel off-centre, but how quickly can you come back to your heart space? Your life purpose manifests by just being your true you and staying true to your alignment.

If you are not of the world, you can't help the world. We are all coming back to our natural design that is a connected heart to the cosmos, with a limited physical structure and mind construct. This limited structure only coming out in a short span of time according to the soul, a laborious or glorious lifetime, depending how we choose to perceive life and we have the power to control our perceptions of the world around us. Human fear has controlled our sacred temple for too long and now the Universe is saying, "No more! It's time to shift the collective consciousness, reconnect to Source and return to the original Soul Blueprint for humanity." It is why so many of you have become awakened. What isn't part of our true blueprint is becoming undone and this can make us feel uncomfortable because our worldly limited perception becomes shattered.

Every moment is leading you to help shift the unnecessary karmic cycles people have been stuck in due to the *Age of the Power of the Mind*. Now, it's coming into the *Age of the Heart*.

It's only through this new paradigm of shifting humanity can we all begin to come back to our original DNA design. As our environment changes, our DNA changes. Our makeup. Every bit we do to help others, even our soul family, we will begin to see that others will no longer have to suffer.

This lifetime has the greatest opportunity for collective change. You may ask, why did I come to Earth when I could've stayed in a space of unconditional love in Spirit? From a soul's perspective you saw a great opportunity. An important gateway into the greatest shift of the collective consciousness. You're more courageous than you think. Your assimilation into the world had to happen so that you could understand how people think and operate. This is a time when people are seeking meditation, yoga and more moments when they can try and find the truth and meaning to life. There's a deep yearning within their being that can hear the muffles of their soul and wanting to hear it more clearly.

You are learning to master your body and mind, so that your Spirit is the one operating at all times. You become a trinity of mind, body and soul working in harmony. You are the living proof that it can be done. You can live a spirited life. You are that living proof that each and every day, the Divine is manifested in every moment. You are that glimmer of hope and peace this world has been waiting for. You are needing to rise, so that others can rise with you. The greatest influencers are those who have learnt how to help inspire and transform others to be the best versions of themselves. Whether you have one follower or one million in your life or on your social media account, the ability to make someone smile, inspired, to feel loved or experience a sense of peace is the gift we give to others. We are all the lighthouses, helping others to find their way. Whatever we experience, helps us to create our structure for our lighthouse. Without the things that 'happened' to us, our ability to seek the light might not have been possible.

You are constantly being initiated into a higher state and new way of being. You know when you've been initiated because you attain an awareness of something to work and shift through. The beauty is as an advanced soul and being your most spirited Self, you've been here before. The only difference is now you have the tools to navigate through whatever life throws at you. You understand on a core level whether you need the time to *integrate, change* or you might be even experiencing a *transitional* period where the only action you can do is wait and focus on filling your cup up. The rewards from the Universe are boundless and we know deep within our hearts that this is the truth and that's what keeps us going. The Universe continues to send us signs and symbols along the way allowing us to know that we are always being guided. Guided to a higher state of be-ing. The good thing is now that we have a soul map to understand what our lessons are, where we might be in the soul cycle and how to navigate and align to our purpose. You have the map to navigate through anything so that the essence of your soul can shine through.

We have to stay committed to the process. Committed to being aligned to the light. This is not for the faint hearted. Can you still maintain your integrity, even when chaos comes? The *Master of One* understands the flow of life. The chaos and beauty that coexist in each and every moment, yet this is what makes it all so unique and special. You have peace of mind and find unconditional love, acceptance, forgiveness or compassion in all that occurs. This is transcendental thinking. The transcendence of human thought forms to divine ways of thinking in a grounded way. Grounded with heart, love and grace. Here in this state, you become unshakable. As we continue to get lighter our sensitivity increases because we are no longer numbing that which doesn't give us fulfilment. We become in-tune with our true feelings and desires.

Light and shadow, love and hurt, all is working out just as it needed to be. Our life is manifested through the Art of Spirit. Flowing, dynamic, vibrant and full of colour. If we choose to see the life that unfolds for us as if it's a masterpiece, we allow the grace of the Divine to flow through more. Knowing that we are the artist and all that happens in our life is the best painting we could ever create, we understand that Spirit is like a mentor, giving tips and signs on how it could be even better if we choose to listen, be still and be open to the unlimited possibilities the Universe has to offer. It is a magical miracle.

The *Master of One* understands that grace underpins all that occurs. Nothing in life is by coincidence and the flow of grace is evident. In grace, no judgement, fear or pain resides. Grace works through everything we can see, feel and touch and all that can't be felt with our senses. The grace of the Divine is present everywhere. All is working out perfectly in divine timing and with purpose in every moment. It occurs when we our awareness expands, our life changes, when we are integrating and even through transitional periods. Grace fills our hearts with gratitude, peace and blessings. Master your life by consciously choosing actions that allow you to be as your most spirited Self. In our most spirited Self, we realise that nothing separates us, that in actual fact we are whole and perfect, even in the imperfect.

The Divine has but no choice to reveal itself, when you believe in it. The flow of the Divine is not reserved for a special someone. It is in all that exists. The more work you do on you and focusing on a transcendental experience, the more we open our heart and mind to see the divine present. You unlock the highest perception possible, seeing through the eyes of the soul. Surrendering to what is and knowing that everything that is happening in each and every moment is perfect and the way it's meant to be. Life is unfolding how it is meant to.

> **You are perfect the way you are.**
> **You are worthy.**
> **You are Divine.**

You co-create a world with the Divine, expressing through your heart, words, actions and experiences. A creator in your own right, choosing to experience more spirited moments with the best version of you. Your purpose is acted out with clarity, conviction and Spirit, knowing deep down what really matters most. As you come to know your True Self, the path is as clear as the crystal blue ocean. Whether you're a stay at home mum, a barista, personal trainer, coach, teacher, blogger, entrepreneur or student, no matter what you do, your life purpose is exactly how it's meant to be from your unique Soul Blueprint, and this can change over time. Your gifts and talents unravel and become illuminated, like the missing puzzle pieces just fit in delightfully in your life. Joy is magnetic and helps to attract synchronistic flow in each and every moment. Aligning to joy is aligning to our most authentic state. Joy is in the journey and what will expand when we choose this as our intentional focus. It can shift any lower thought forms to fall away and allow what you truly want to expand.

Your mastery brings grace to life for others. For people who have their minds closed are looking for where the Divine might be present. Acting as an agent of the Divine, you become a sign for others to open up and connect to a presence that's there for them too. You light up their life to be more of who they are and for them to experience more love, joy and blessings. The divine blueprint being manifested in physical form. Your highest Soul Blueprint becomes activated.

You become the divine being present, but you can only do so if you consciously choose to be of both worlds. As we open up our hearts to a deeper divine presence, this is how we become an instrument of peace. We expand and become undoubtedly connected with the cosmos becoming knowingly plugged into something that can't be put into words. The entire cosmos existing within and around us. In every person we see, in all that we touch. The seen and unseen. All that entices our senses and beyond. The possible and beyond the impossible. We can feel this divine presence all around us. Graceful. Endless. Boundless. The only way to stay in this state is to stay open. Stay open to experiencing the Divine and to receive its blessings. The more open we are, the more we allow lower thought forms and suffering to release. It dissipates. With each moment we courageously choose to live from the heart space, we learn to see life like we've never seen it before. We unlearn life as we once knew it and begin to experience living our true spirited life. We are learning how to balance perfectly like on a tightrope the integration of your divine Self to become a master of your destiny—The *Master of One*.

You are worthy.
You are whole.
You are one.

SOUL MAP

The *Soul Map* guides you to fully integrate your new knowledge and discover where your soul is guiding you. In this ritual you will activate your innate clear sight, your purpose and what your soul is here to do. True Alignment manifesting in its divine order.
Everything will begin to unfold, layer upon layer, image upon image.

We are all being called.
We are being called to step into our Light.

You are learning to master your life back from the power of your soul.
You are learning SOUL MASTERY.
You are the *master of one.*

The Soul Map is a full integration.

INITIATION

She is the one who has been awakened by the Universe in divine timing. She is ready to be birthed. She is belonging to something greater than herself and starting the venture of self-discovery.

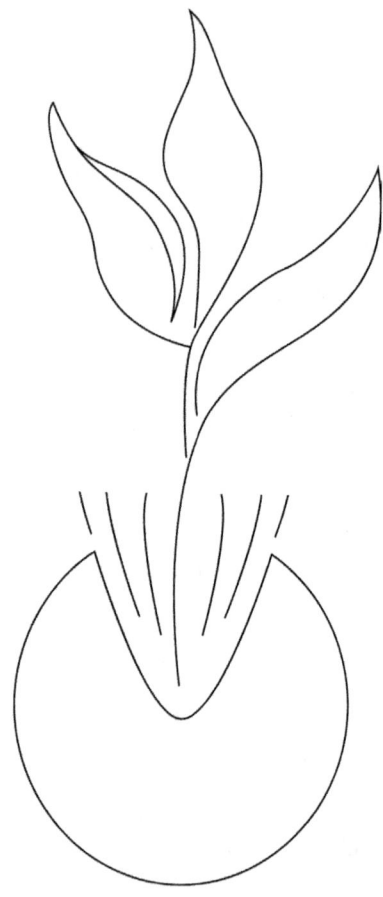

Soul Map Image 1

**INITIATION. BIRTH. BREAKING ILLUSIONS.
HEART AWAKENING.
NEW CYCLE. NEW BEGINNINGS.**

AWAKENING

She is the one who is awakened, questioning her life with a new awareness. She is beginning to feel that her life has changed and things that were once a part of her no longer resonate with her any longer. She may experience deep pain, suffering, dark night of the soul vibes. She becomes the seeker.

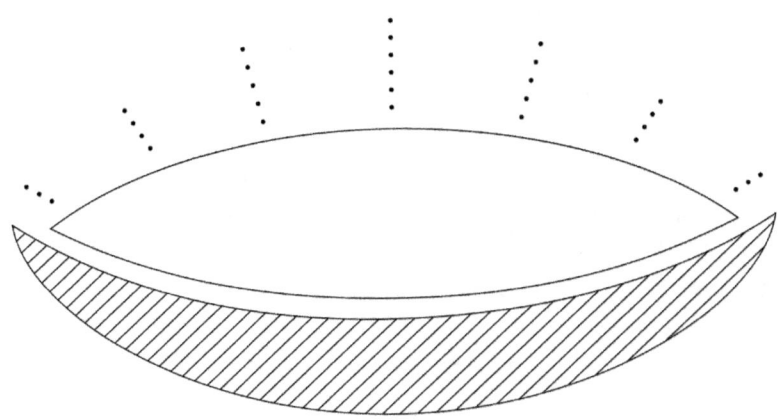

Soul Map Image 2

AWARENESS. DEEP. ILLUMINATION.

TRANSITION

She is going through a deep transformational period where she is becoming clearer about her alignment and is beginning to receive the biggest shift in her life. She begins to find the changes she needs to do in order to follow her soul and starts to listen to her intuition and tune in with what needs to leave.

Soul Map Image 3

SHADOW. SHIFTS. FAITH. SURRENDER.

CHANGE AND INTEGRATION

She is the one that knows what's needed in order to follow her own path and begin to make the necessary changes that are for her highest good but in order for her to live a life congruent from her soul. She will need to allow time for it to integrate. Failure to change is to be stuck in a continuous cycle.

Soul Map Image 4

CHANGE. INTEGRATE. COURAGE. MOVEMENT.

TRANSCENDENCE

She is the one who lives from the heart. She has worked through the lessons and has found the blessings. She is living a life of soul. Fully in her power. If she hasn't mastered a particular lesson she will go through the cycle and be initiated again because a deeper learning transcends.

Soul Map Image 5

**ALCHEMY. DEEPER PURPOSE. CONNECTED.
HEIGHTENED INTUITION. POWER.**

SELF-ACTUALISATION

She is the one in this lifetime meant for big things and can see her presence as being an expression of the Divine. She is owning her power and soul is the only place she works from. She is of service. Divine potentiality.

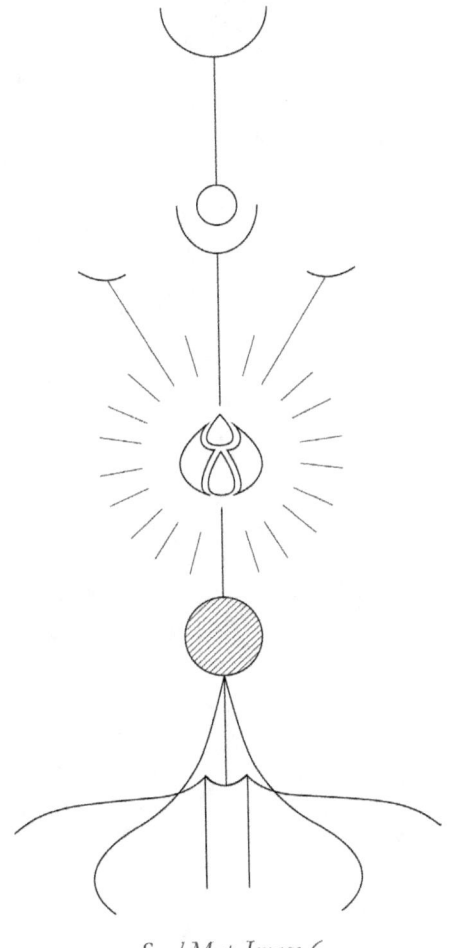

Soul Map Image 6

EMBODIMENT. MASTERY. DIVINE. GRACE. SOUL.

SOUL MAP

She is the *master of one, of herself, fully.*

SOUL MASTERY. COMPLETION.

ACKNOWLEDGEMENTS

Firstly, Spirit, thank you for guiding me to write this and showing up each and every time. This book surprised me and showed me the power of trust and faith in the Universe. You ignited the quest to find out more about the mysteries of the universe and you always seemed to give the inspiration I needed to write.

To Michelle, thanks for always believing in me and pushing me to keep following my dream, to just keep writing and making me feel that I can do anything I put my mind to.

To Stacey, thanks for keeping me sane, showing me how to stay authentically aligned to Spirit, even when it seemed as if it was a struggle to get through everything. I have never met such a strong soul and you give hope to so many.

To Alex, Conor, Susan, Tess, Amy, Ally and Cynthia, for reminding me of the magic that exists and to keep following my dream. You made the path lighter.

To Fil, thanks for your guidance along the way. Your authenticity and wisdom are such gifts to the world. You always helped me to see the light, when it felt impossible to see. You are a big light to this world.

To my teacher and mentor, Rebecca Campbell. For teaching me how to stay aligned to my soul and to stay committed to my path. When I've doubted my abilities, I can constantly hear your words of encouragement and it allowed me to keep going. Your words to 'stick to one creative idea' helped me to actually complete a book! Thank you for being you.

To Lisa Williams, thanks for helping me to lift the veil on being true to myself always. You are such a gift to the world; you always seem to pop up when I need a guiding light. Thank you for divine wisdom and honesty always.

To all the staff at Tinker café, thanks for keeping me caffeinated, focused and dedicated to completing this book.

To the Sacred Keys team, you are such a light to this world. Thanks for being an incredible loving and supportive soul family. It was the platform for my awakening, growth and learning. All the practitioners and workshop facilitators were the perfect blend for not only me, but others to feel a deeper connection to something greater. The keys to the heart and gateway to the Divine.

To Alana and Lydia, thanks for all the laughs and our crazy psychedelic chats. You make the 'crazy' feel normal.

To Jess Lee Williams, thank you for saying 'Yes' to illustrating this book. You make this book complete through your sacred work. You are a beautiful, radiant light in this world and I'm so grateful for you entering my life when you did. You were exactly what I put out to the Universe. As soon as I received all the graphics, my heart smiled. Thank you.

To Natasha Gilmour, my divine editor and publisher. There's no doubt from the moment that we connected that I knew that it was not only synchronistical but destiny. The Divine was definitely at play. Thank you for maintaining the integrity and soul of this book. You are truly a gift to this world. Your magic and support helped me to make my dream come true. For this, I'm eternally grateful for. Thank you to Elle Lynn for her incredible work to pull this all together, and make this book look purely divine.

To all my dear family, friends, supporters and teachers, thank you for all your love and support.

To everyone I have crossed paths with, there's never no coincidences in life. I am grateful for the impact you have made on my life.

Finally, a big thanks to you, the reader! Thank you for taking time to be on this journey with me. I wish for you many blessings! Continue to be the light.

ABOUT THE AUTHOR

Jacqueline Teej is a writer, inspirational speaker, teacher and coach. Her passion for life and quest for transformation led her to complete many workshops and courses dedicated to her spiritual awakening journey. This included Reiki mastership, sacred soul guidance, astrology, tarot, IIN health coaching and rocking out at *Spirit Junkie* masterclasses. She has worked as a devoted holistic therapist, utilising all her skillset to help clients on their path. Furthermore, she offers her unique experience of holistic health and working as a teacher to assist others with finding and aligning to their true self.

Jacqueline is passionate about inspiring others to live a life from the heart, trust their intuition and align to their absolute highest calling. She has worked with, and been mentored by, key leaders in the spiritual industry such as Alana Fairchild, Lisa Williams and Rebecca Campbell.

Instagram @jacquelineteej
Facebook: jacquelineteej
Website: jacquelineteej.com

www.ingramcontent.com/pod-product-compliance
Lightning Source LLC
Chambersburg PA
CBHW050304010526
44107CB00055B/2103